Fast Moving Consumer Goods

FMCG's

Designed

To Help

Salesforce

&

Business Owners

By

Mohammed K. Hamidaddin

Mohammed K. Hamidaddin
Graduated From
George Washington University
In The USA
With
MSc & Degree
Of Engineer
In Engineering Management
Experience

Worked For Prominent Multinationals
In Different Countries
For More Than 25 Years

© Mohammed k. Hamidaddin , 2020
King Fahd National Library
Cataloging-in-Publication Data

Hamidaddin, Mohammed K.
FMCGs Guideline Hand-Book.
/ Mohammed K. Hamidaddin
.- Jeddah , 2020
132p ; ..cm
ISBN: 978-603-03-4776-6
1- sales I-Title
658.81 dc 1441/12710
L.D. no. 1441/12710
ISBN: 978-603-03-4776-6

CONTENT

Preface	1
Introduction To FMCG's.	1
The Eight Principles Of FMCG's **Categories.**	5
1-Category Management Principle #1 Covers (A-F Items).	6
A-**Category Definition**	7
B-**Category Role & Responsibility**	7
C-**Category Appraisal**	8
D-**Category Score-Card**	9
E-**Category Strategy** (I-VI Items)	10
F-**How To Grow The Market Share?**	11

II-**How To Accelerate The Sales Of WTO's?**	11
III-**How To Increase Foot Traffic?**	12
IV-**How To Improve Gross Margin?**	13
V-**How To Increase Return On Investment ROI?**	13

VI-How To Increase The Shopping Basket Size?	14
F-Category Tactics + Category Plan And Review.	15
G-Category Market Feedback	16
2-Category Operation Management Principle #2 (Covers A-E Items)	19
A)-Customer Development Tasks And Responsibilities	20
B)-Achieve Sales Growth For All Categories	21

C)-How To Create Demand For A Product?	22
D)-How To Launch A New Product?	23
E)-How To Augment Demand For A Product Known To Consumers? (I-VI Items)	24
I-On Pack Promotion	24
II-Getting Rebate	24
III-Run Trade Drive	25
IV-Provide A Redeem Scheme	26

V-Use Brand Supply Shortage	26
VI-Use Of TV Commercials	27

3-Marketing Mix Of 4P's Principle #3 Covers A-C Items	30
A-The Industrial Model Of The Marketing Mix Of 4P's	30
Product	31
Price	33
Place	34
Promotion	35
B-The Industrial Model Of The Marketing Mix Of 4P's-Summary	39
C -The Service Model Of The Marketing Mix Of 3P's.	40
People	40
What Qualification Should FMCG's Salesman have?	41
Process	42
Physical Evidence	43

4-Customer Marketing Covers (A-F) Principle #4	**46**
A-What Is Customer Marketing?	47
B-How To Grow Current Winning Trade Outlets WTO's?	48
C-Segmenting Consumer Market	49
Demographic	49
Geographic	50
Psychographic	50
Behavioral	51
D-Customer Marketing Guideline And Strategy	51
E-How To Increase The Sales & Profit Of WTO's?	52
F-How To Develop In Market/Instore Activities	53

5-Visibility And Merchandising (Principle #5)	**55**
A-Job To Be Done Daily At Winning Trade Outlets WTO's	56

B-The Power Of Merchandising	57
C-The Power Of Sampling	58
D-The Power Of Outstanding Displays	59
E-Use The Following Tactics When Launching A New Product (A-F)	60
F-Selling Shelf Space	61
G-How To Reduce Out Of Stock?	62
H-How To Improve Shelf Space Inventory?	63
I-What Is Share Of Shelf	64
J-Visibility & Merchandising Guideline Strategy	65
6-Routes To Markets Principle #6	**67**
A-What Is Routes To Market?	68
B-Market Structure-Example	68
C-Coverage Strategy	69
D-Sales Strategy Coverage	72

E-How To Achieve Effective Direct Coverage	74
F-How To Select Winning Trade Outlets WTO's?	75
G-What Is Numeric & Weighted Coverage?	76
H-Sales Strategy Coverage Continues	77
I-The Frequency Of The Coverage Of WTO's	79
J-What Is An Efficient Coverage?	79
K-The Company's Branches	80
L- Branch Scorecard	83
N-Retail Van Salesman Scorecard	85
O-Setting Targets For Retail Van Salesman- Bill Productivity BP	86
P-Setting Targets For Retail Van Salesman Bill Productivity BP **Continues**	87
Q-Line Per Productive Call LPPC.	89
R- How To Secure 100% Outcome For BP & LPPC?	94
7-Win With Winning Trade Outlets Principle #7	**96**
A-How To Win With Winning Outlets WTO's?	99

B-How To Prepare Sales Strategy?	100
C-What Is Share Of Shelf? SOS?	100
D-How To Prepare Joint Business Plan? - JBP	100
E-How To Develop Growth Strategy For? JBP	101
F-What Is Joint Business Plan Scorecard?	102

Shoppers & Consumers Insights Principle # 8	**104**
A-Shoppers Insights	105
B-Understand The Below Factors To Achieve Success.	105
C-What Are The Stimulus To Create A Purchase?	105
D-Shoppers Insights – Turning Shoppers Into Buyers	106
E-How To Turn Shoppers Into Buyers?	106
F-Who Is The Consumer?	107

G-Understanding Consumer Insight	107
H-What Are The Objectives Of Shoppers/Retailers/And Brand Owners?	108

Preparing An Activity Proposal Example	
A1-Activity Proposal Number	110
A2-Date Of The Activity	110
A3-The Budget Of The Activity	110
B-The Objective Of The Activity	110
B1-Achieve 12% Growth	110
B2-Attain 100% Coverage Of WTO's	110
B3-Get 100% Availability Of Key SKU's	110
C-The Mechanic Of The Activity	110
D-Cost Of The Activity	113
E-Detail Of The Cost	114
F- Monitoring Of The Activity	115

<u>Preface</u>

For Fast Moving Consumer Goods FMCGs business to sustain growth and achieve an attractive return on investment ROI, it must have the ability to endure growth, adapt, innovates, be reliable, creative, be friendly with the environment and establish a productive win-win relationship with key customers.

It is profoundly vital to learn the business know-how of FMCGs to achieve fertile results and accomplish outstanding growth.

Competition is getting tougher and smarter and for the business to win in the market it has to have superior creativity, outstanding leadership, and exhibit strong follow up constantly.

In the world of FMCGs business, prevailing issues such as poor customer service, customers' orders' delivery not on time nor according to their purchase orders, low availability and crappy visibility of key brands in important Winning Trade Outlets WTO's in addition to the pathetic managing of limited financial resources are problems facing the business every day.

In my 27 years of experience in the industry in different countries, I have realized that there are a need and demand for a simple guideline handbook on FMCGs specifying tasks and responsibilities of the sales-force aiming to accomplish greater success and driving sustainable and solid growth for the business.

<u>Introduction To FMCG's</u>

The products that you shop at a grocery outlet in your neighborhood to fulfill your daily needs are called Fast Moving Consumer Goods FMCG's. The gain from selling FMCG's in small quantities is small. However, when those products are sold in huge basketful, the profit is massive. An

example of those products by category is reflected in the below table.

Home and Personal Care Categories

Skin Care	Fabric Wash
Personal Care	Home Care
Hair Care	Toilet Tissues
Oral Care	Paper Products
Talcum	House Cleaners
Deodorants	Shoe Care
Cosmetics	
Perfume	

<u>Process Foods Categories</u>

Ice Creams	Juices
Baker Products	Coffee
Cereals	Bottles Waters
Chocolates	Vegetables
Snack Food	Sugar
Soft Drinks	Rice
Tea	Dairy Products
Health Beverages	Confectionary

In addition to the above categories, products such as below categories are also regarded as FMCG's:

1-Plastic goods	5- Consumer Electronics
2-Stationery	6- Plastic
3- Pharmaceuticals,	
4- perfumeries	

References
1-Channel trading basics – Daily FX
https://www.dailyfx.com/forex/.../trading_tips/...of.../Channel_Trading_Basics.html
2-Channel Trading Strategy Guide - Forex Channel Trading System
https://tradingstrategyguides.com/rabbit-trail-channel-trading-strategy/
3-Understanding Distribution Channel –Lynda.com
https://www.lynda.com/Business.../Understanding-distribution-channels/.../188148-4.h...
4-Distribution Channels In Marketing: Definition, Types, and Examples
https://study.com/.../distribution-channels-in-marketing-definition-t...
5- What is FMCG?
https://jobs.telegraph.co.uk/article/what-is-fmcg
6-FMCG definition and meaning Collins English Dictionary
https://www.collinsdictionary.com/dictionary/english/fmcg 7-
14 Examples of FMCG – Simplicable
https://simplicable.com/new/fmcg
8-FMCG: The Power Of Fast Moving Consumer Goods
https://www.amazon.com/FMCG-Power-Fast-Moving-Consumer-Goods/.../16228764.
9-Fast Moving Consumer Goods – Wikipedia
https://en.wikipedia.org/wiki/Fast-moving_consumer_goods
10-Five Habit of Successful Retailers.
https://www.forbes.com/sites/nicoleleinbachreyhlefive-habits-successful-retailers/
11-The Seven **Habit** of Highly Successful Retailers
https://www.shopify.com/retail/7-good-habits-of-highly-successful-retailers
12-Top 10 FMCG Companies.
https://www.mbaskool.com/.../top.../17186-top-10-fmcg-companies-in-the-world-201...
13-Top 100 Consumer Goods Companies 2017
https://consumergoods.com/top-100-consumer-goods-companies-2017
14-The Hunt 100-The Top Consumer Goods Companies - 2017
https://www.slideshare.net/.../the-hunt-100-the-top-consumer-goods-companies-2007-

The Eight Principles of FMCG's Categories

There are more than 30 **categories of Fast Moving Consumer Goods** FMCGs. **To build up and to accomplish sustainable growth for the business, It is highly imperative to comprehend the principles of** FMCG's in great detail. **Understanding and implementing the Eight Principles of** FMCG's **is extremely important to achieve massive success in the world of** FMCG **business.**

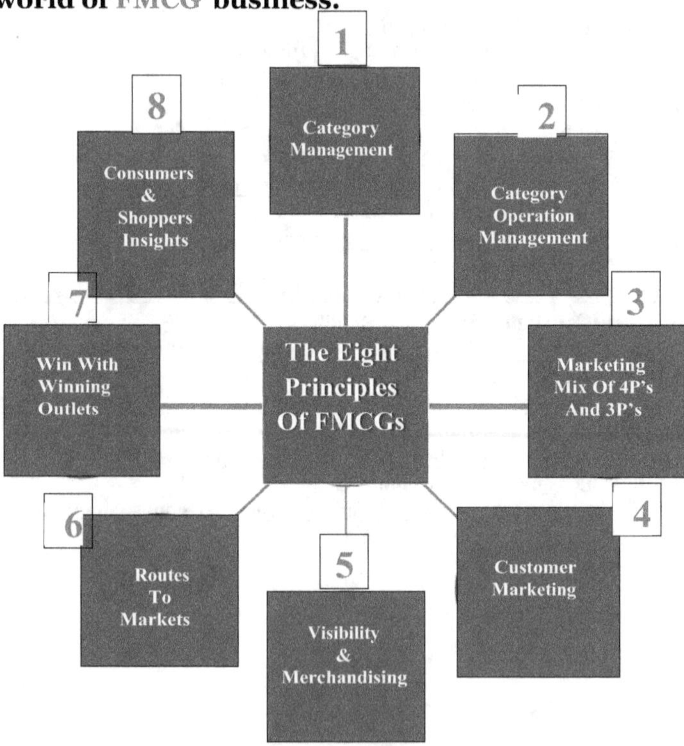

The primary objective of every company large or small is to manage its business successfully, achieve the target year on year, obtain higher market shares, secure sustainable growth, offer attractive Return On Investment ROI **to investors, and be friendly with the environment. For the company to reach such an important** goal successfully**, it has to understand and implement the** eight **principles of the** FMCG's perfectly **and make them work in coordination and harmony with each other as one unit across all the functions of the eight principles of** FMCG's**.**

1-Category Management Principle # 1

Category Management Covers The Following Topics (A-G).

A-**Category Definition**

B-**Category Role**

C-**Category Appraisal**

D-**Category Score Card**

E-**Category Strategy with the aim to achieve:**
 -Grow Market Share
 -Increase The Sales Of Important
  Customers (WTO's)
 -Increase Growth Margin
 -Increase Return On Investment ROI
 -Increase Foot Traffic @ Targeted Customers'
  Outlets.

F-**Category Tactics**

G-**Category Plan & Review**

<u>A)-Category Definition</u>

I- FMCGs **such as milk, toilet papers, soft drinks, food items, detergents, fabric softeners, hair care, oral care, cosmetics, and others** are divided into categories **to manage them effectively.**

II- **Trade channels display the same category products alongside each other on the shelves** based on sameness and similarities **with consumer tastes, preferences, and dislikes. The aim is to make it easy for consumers and shoppers to buy them and thus accelerate their growth.**

III- **The products are categorized and arranged by assortment, by pack sizes and displayed next to each other. It is vital to make shopping easy and convenient for consumers and shoppers to stimulate them to buy your products and become your regular customers.**

<u>B)-Category **Role & Responsibility**</u>

1- **The category role is to build the category, achieve growth, and increase its market shares.**

2- **To establish outstanding visibility leadership** at POP **and build attractive superior floor displays to influence shoppers and consumers to buy displayed products to generate revenue and increase profit.**

3- **To provides the right assortment at a competitive price and encounter competitors' prices.**

4- **To ensure** 100% **availability of the category and offer lots of promotions on the category every month and events.**

5- **Assure delivery orders of customers on time as per their orders and minimize the timing of loading and unloading.**

6- **Understand shoppers and consumers' buying habits to increase the category's sales and market shares.**

7- **The category management should liquidate slow-moving items and take back the expiry. This is important to encourage more trade investment in the category.**

8- **The category should use** TV **commercials to enhance awareness and announces sales occasions on events to create excitements and generate higher sales for the category**

9- **The category should contract shelf space at** WTO's **for allowing more facing visibility for the category at the point of purchase to generate higher sales & profit.**

10- **The category should offer all kinds of promotions to reward regular users of the category. It should also do sampling with gifts to bring more users to the category.**

C)-Category Appraisal

1- **Do a weekly analysis of the market position of the category in comparison to competitors.**

2- **Scrutinize the market share of the category against the competitors every month.**

3- **Examine the strengths of the category in the market in terms of growth versus competitors.**

4- **Explore the** opportunities **available for the category to** grow **and what is needed to be done to increase its market share?**

5- **Evaluate the category in terms of availability, visibility, in-store activities, resources, assortment, packaging, responding to the delivery of customers' orders, customers' satisfaction, and overall product relative issues and services.**

6- **Get** trade **feedback from the market and key** WTO's **on the category performance vs competitors in to obtain a better picture on the category in the market.**

D)- Category Scorecard-KPI

Every Category or annual budget must have a Scorecard to measure its performance against set targets. See the below figure. Such measurement is called (Key Performance Indicator) or KPI which gives us a clear way to evaluate market performance results, provide directions, give us a set of facts and feedback to compare results on set targets, and let us understand how we are doing against our competitors and set targets. It is recommended to plan and adjust your budget against KPI market evaluation results to ensure performance efficiency.

D)-Category Scorecard Graph-Example

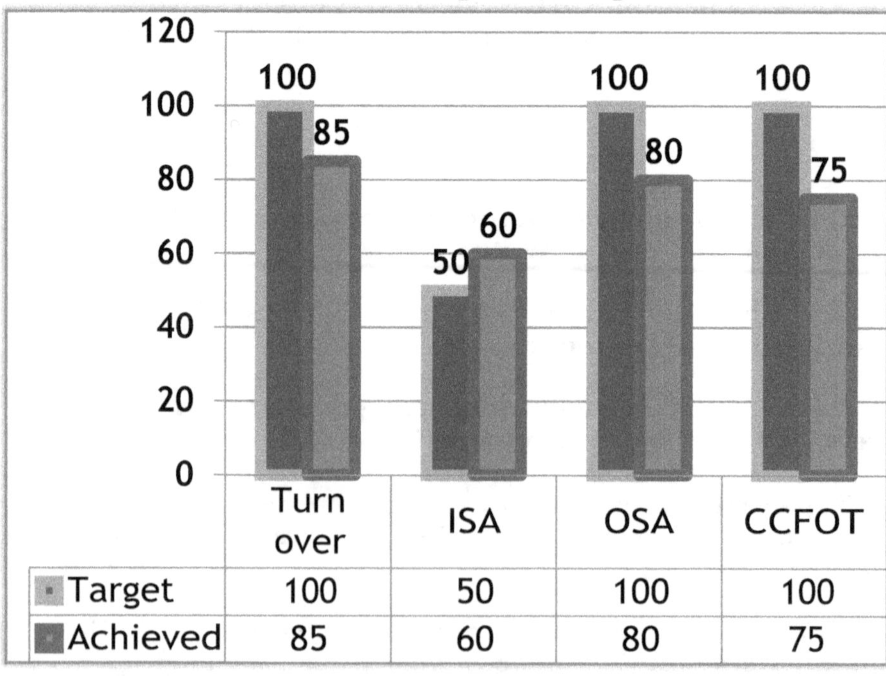

Even though more money was spent on In-store activities ISA, The above figure shows that targets were not achieved due to the poor performance of on-shelf availability OSA, and CCFOT customer case fills on time both are critical for achieving set targets.

The category strategy aims to achieve the following important requirements I-VI:

I-Grow the market share of the category. Set a target for example by 10% over the previous year.

II-Increase the sales of WTO's, for example by 20% over the previous year via providing them with lots of promotions and in-store activities.
Secure delivering their orders on time and as stated in the purchase orders. Ensure superior customer service.

III-Augment foot traffic by providing attractive sales activities for shoppers and consumers. Announce one per week for higher discounts on selected items.

IV-Improves gross margin by 10% over last year.

V-Offer a 10% return on investment ROI for investors.

VI-Run-in store activates at WTO's to augment basket size of shoppers and consumers.

I- How To Grow The Market Share?

Set a target to grow your market shares and design the strategy to achieve the set target. If the brand market share increases, it is a sign that the brand strategy is working. The brand is taking sales from competitors.
On the contrary, if the brand market share is declining, this is an indication that the brand is losing sales to its competitors, and action must be taken to amend the strategy.

The brand is losing market shares because the strategy is not providing the right direction for growth. Review strategy and take the following course of action:

Secure strong availability of fast-moving brands, ensure leadership at POP, construct outstanding floor displays, increase TV commercials, do sampling at key important outlets, come up with innovations, and provide attractive stimulus offering valuable gifts, lots of promotions for consumers and shoppers to increase their purchase.

You should bear in mind that Key WTO's prefer to invest in brands with high market shares because they can get back their investment on the brands quicker with a good margin.

II- How to Accelerate the sales of WTO's?

a)-Establish a professional customer development team that is highly trained to drive vigorous sales schemes based on market knowledge and provide the right schemes, and in-market events, sampling with attractive gifts.

b)-Develop a salesforce with a sense of urgency to follow up with WTO's orders. The sales-force must possess the knowledge and the ability to engage and to establish an outstanding relationship with WTO's based on a win-win outcome.

c-Create an excellent and impressive merchandising team to execute outstanding visibility at POP across key winning trade outlets WTO's. Use attractive and good quality of POSM to communicate the benefit of the brands to shoppers. Construct TV screens in key WTO's showing commercial videos of the brands to influence shoppers to pick up the company's brands and buy them.

d-Help WTO's outlets to liquidate slow-moving pack sizes and take back expiry date.

e-Make sure that your brands possess attractive packaging, and sufficient support to offer various promotions to increase sales and encounter competitors in the market.

III- How To Increase Foot Traffic?

a)-Get beautiful in-store layout design, attractive wide shelf space, well-organized racks, fixtures, and walls.

b)-Make the store clean, neat, organized, and has a nice environment. The outlet should have good lighting, a fresh atmosphere with air conditioning. Install fresh fruit, bakery, meats, and other essential sections. Offer lots of promotions on various and number of brands.

c)-Set a day per week offering a discount on valuable items. Arrange an especial floor area with attractive and organized displays that should be allocated for the discounted items.

d)-Secure 100% availability of fast-moving brands. Increase the facing of packs with a high margin. Use special TV screen banners in the store to communicate events, and promotions available in the store. Make shoppers get the sense of being winners in your store.

IV- How To Improve Gross Margin?

a)-Minimize the cost of goods sold from sales revenue to increase gross profit.

b)-Cutdown the overhead and introduce new technology to produce products at less cost. Minimize waste and maximize the skill of workers. Source better cost for raw material. Increase the efficiency of the operation to 95% or higher.

c)-Enhance the skill of the workforce by offering more training to accelerate output and trim down outage.

d)-Offer incentives based on a margin of profit to employees to increase their Bill Productivity (BP) and Line Per Productive Call LPPC.

IV- How To Improve Gross margin Continue? Example

Sales Revenue ....$ 523,000
Cost Of Goods Sold ......$ 325,000
Gross Profit....................$ 198,000
Total Expenses ....$ 100,000
Earning Before Tax...... $ 98,000
Tax.....................................
$ 35,000
Net Earning....................$ 63,000
Gross Margin = $198,000/$523,000X100=38%

The above example shows that bringing down the cost of goods sold would increase the gross profit and net earnings.

V- How To Increase Return On Investment ROI?

a-Increase Bill Productivity BP of the market visit and maximize Line Per Productive Call LPPC to a higher focus on coverage and distribution of WTO's. The aim is to generate high revenue for all items on sales to reduce the inventory

cost of the stock in the company's warehouses and also, reduce the cost of the operation to achieve attractively ROI.

b-Secure higher sales of fast-moving SKUs with a good margin. Reduce Time of Invoicing, loading, and unloading to the lowest possible time level standard. Be efficient across all functions. Generally, investors are interested to invest in companies with a strong financial background to secure their ROI. For this, companies increase their efficiency by reducing their running operational costs as well as minimizing the cost of production materials.

c-Investors seek a better return on investment so they can get a higher ROI available in the market. For this, investors minimize risk by scrutinizing periodical financial results of financial institutions where they desire to invest in them.

VI- How To Increase The Shopping Basket Size?

a-Shoppers and consumers prefer to find their needs in one outlet under one roof. They make a trip to an outlet & expect to find fully their needs. Stock WTO's with the right products with the right assortment. Ensure to establish leadership visibility at the POP.

b-Winning Trade outlets WTO's have to understand consumers' and shoppers' demands. Their stock management is based on prevailing consumer demands. The company should help them to achieve this end objective with strong follow up and great support.

c- WTO's should allow the highly demanded brands to establish leadership at the POP to achieve higher sales and profit. The company should also secure the shelf space contract signed with WTO's on a daily follow up by sales-force and merchandisers.

d-To increase shopping basket size, WTO's need to make shoppers and consumers spend more time in their outlets to

buy more products. This can be done by offering good
lighting, a nice atmosphere, and lots of promotions.
It is important to create an attractive layout of the outlet
with a friendly environment, illumination, organized shelves,
cleanliness, and massive floor displays with attractive POPM.
Sampling with gifts can be used to incentivize shoppers and
consumers to increase their purchase, buy new products, and
spend more time in the outlet. Offer massive promotions on
health and body care products. The aim is to incentivize
shoppers to buy beauty products that have a high margin.

e-On seasonal occasions, incentivize shoppers, and
consumers by offering valuable and attractive promotions on
key brands. Make Massive displays for promoted brands on
the POP to influence shoppers to buy displayed brands. Do
monthly or weekly events so shoppers and consumers get
used to the habit to visit your outlet to take advantage of the
regular events and discounts.

F-Category Tactics

First, do a SWOT analysis to reach clarity on what is needed
for the category to introduce superior tactical schemes
against competitors and to win in the market.

Second, assist retail outlets to liquidate their slow stock by
offering tactical schemes on slow-moving brands and packs.
This would build trust and encourage trade to invest more in
the company's brands.

Third, offer attractive promotions on events and occasions to
bring more users to the category. Make shoppers and
consumers feel that they win by purchasing your brands
perceived as good value for money.

Fourth, Secure 100% availability of the right assortment to
make it easy for shoppers to pick up the brands. Go for
massive floor displays at key locations at WTO's.

1- Aim

a)-**Get Clear Picture Of The Category Position VS Competitors In The Market Before Planning.**
b)-**Do Complete SWOT Analysis On The Competitors performance VS Your Brands Performance.**

2- Action

a)-**Ensure 100% Availability of Fast Moving Packs.**
b)-**Introduce Powerful Tactical Schemes & Leadership Visibility.**
c)-**Secure Financial Resources.**

3-Achieve

a)-**Higher Sales**
b)-**Higher Growth**
c)-**Higher Market Shares**
d)-**Higher Customer Service**

Category Market Feedback

To ensure successful results on planning and review, the following actions are strongly recommended:

a-Get feedback on how was the category perfuming against set targets? If the results were not according to the plan, ensure vigorous execution of the marketing mix elements (Product, Price, Place, Promotion) related to your business and make sure that your routs to markets (RTM) followed by your sales-force are productive and efficient.

b-Make Certain that the category is producing profits to customers as well as for the company as well. It is vital to secure a relationship with WTO based on a Win-Win relationship.

c-Secure visibility leadership at POP with attractive POSM. Ensure 100% availability of fast-moving packs and variants with attractive margins.

d-Provide lots of promotions, tactical schemes, in-store activities to keep consumers connected to your brands.

References

1- Category definition and meaning.
https://www.collinsdictionary.com/dictionary/english/category
2-Category meaning in the Cambridge English Dictionary.
https://dictionary.cambridge.org/dictionary/english/category 3-
Category-Definition of Category by Merriam – Webster
https://www.merriam-webster.com/dictionary/category
4- The 5 most popular roles at retail.
www.newhope.com/blog/5-most-popular-roles-retail
5- Effective Category Management depends on the role of the category.
https://www.sciencedirect.com/science/article/pii/S0022435901000458
6- The Strategic Importance of Category Role in Category Management.
https://www.linkedin.com/.../strategic-importance-category-roles-management-kyle-d... 7-
Consumer Product Category Appraisal and Sensory Experts
https://www.pk-research.com/category-appraisal/
8-Learning from the completion through category appraisal: one
https://onlinelibrary.wiley.com/doi/full/10.1046/j.1471-5740.2001.00011.x
9-Category Management in Retail Scorecard
https://blog.cmkg.org/blog/http/blog.../scorecard_category-management-in-retail_02
10-Category Management in Retail Scorecard: Compare part 3 results
https://blog.cmkg.org/blog/category-management-in-retail-scorecard-compare-part-3
11-Category Strategy Development & implementation.
https://www.slideshare.net/scimex/category-strategy-development-implementation
12-6 Merchandising Strategies that Increase Category Sales.
https://www.dotactiv.com/blog/6-merchandising-strategies-that-increase-category-sales
13-What is category management?
https://www.dotactiv.com/what-is-category-management
14-Category: Tactics
https://en.wikipedia.org/wiki/Category:Tactics
15-Category Management Tactics
https://www.emeraldinsight.com/doi/10.1108/09590550610667065
16- Category Planning Process
https://www.cips.org/.../Category%20Planning%20Process%20SA%20CIPSA%20Pres
17-Category Management – Wikipedia
https://en.wikipedia.org/wiki/Category_management
18-Category Planning
https://www.efficioconsulting.com/en-gb/e-flow-technology/category-planning/
19-Gross margin
https://en.wikipedia.org/wiki/Gross_margin
20-Gross margin—Best Definition
www.investinganswers.com/financial-dictionary/financial.../gross-margin-2208

Category Operation Management Covers the Following Topics (A-E).

A-Customer Development Management Which Has The Following Tasks And Responsibilities:
1-To secure 100% Availability Of The Important Brands.
2-To Insure visibility leadership @ POP for key brands.
3-To develop precise and sufficient Trade Marketing investment to cover all promotions, and in-store activities at important outlets WTO's
4-To provide forecast by brand by pack size for all brands.
5-To get Needed Resources To Achieve Sales Targets.
6- To develop Activity Planner For The Year (Jan-December)
7- To-the Develop The Skill And Capability Of Sales Force.

B-Achieve Sales Growth For All Categories.

C-Create Demand For All Products.

D-Launch A New Product.

E-Increase Demand For A Product Known To Consumers by using:
On Pack Promotion, Trade Drive, Rebate, Redemption, and TV Commercials

<u>A)-Customer Development (CD) Important Tasks And responsibilities</u>:

A1-Secure 100% availability **of the fast-moving** SKU's **by pack sizes, by variants in Winning Trade outlets** WTO's.

A2-Insure leadership visibility **at the point of purchase POP for important brands by key packs and variants and create massive superior floor displays in prominent locations at** WTO's. **This can be arranged by signing visibility contracts with** WTO's.

A3-Develop precise and sufficient **trade marketing investment to cover all promotions, and in-store activities at** WTO's.

A4)-Provide forecast for individual key outlets **by brand, by pack size, by variants for all targeted brands.**

A5)-Get needed resources **to achieve sales targets and establish a solid sustainable growth, coverage, and distribution.**

A6)-Design activity planner **for individual** WTO's **by month and by quarter.**

A7)-Develop the skill, capability of the sales force **to carry out an efficient route to a market journey cycle and to achieve** WTO's **customers' satisfaction.**

B)-Achieve sales growth for all categories.

Every week, **Category Operation Management organizes a meeting with the Marketing, Customer Development (CD) team and supply chain (SC) to review, coordinate, and evaluate the category sales performance against set targets and encounter competitors if needed.**

The objective is to provide full support, coordination by all functions to secure revenue against set targets and to encounter market challenges posed by the competitors. It is important to achieve sales growth in case of deviation from the set targets and market shares.

The tasks and responsibilities of Customer Development CD, Marketing, and Supply Chain are to achieve success for the company's brands and to face challenges posed by competitors. They should work as one unit to achieve sales growth for all categories. Marketing, customer development, and supply chain. Their mission is to respond vigorously and successfully to fulfill the following vital inquiries:

1- Demand
Is Created By Marketing.

2- Sales
Sales activities are developed by Customer Development CD.

3- Stocks
Is supplied by the supply chain.

C-How To Create Demand For A Product?

C1-Business companies introduce a product to the market and use influential marketing methods such as massive displays, at POP with glamour POSM and attractive packaging. Those companies use TV commercials, promotions, visibility, events, sampling In-store activities to create excitement and demand for the product.

C2-Once the product is launched, it is vital to secure strong coverage and distributors. Sales-force, merchandisers must ensure that the new product is 100% available across important trade channels WTO's.

C3- The new product must be communicated using all methods such as TV commercials, and other means to influence consumers, shoppers, and trade to buy the product. Use lots of promotions as the power of promotion make shoppers buy the new product even if there is a product displayed next to it is better. Consumers and shoppers are attracted to discounted and price-off promotions.

C4-It is important to communicate promoted or discounted brands with clear signs so consumers and shoppers so they can see the offer. Use especial tags to convey the message.

C5-The power of awareness influence you to buy a product you are not aware of it. Consequently, it is important to create high and intensive adverarence for new products to secure purchases and generate high sales and revenue.

C6-TV commercials increase awareness and create demand for a product.

C7-Supermarkets outstanding visibility at POP and massive displays, leaflets, and attractive POSM influence demand and purchase.

C8)-Communications on social media enhance awareness and create demand

C9-Sampling in key outlets has a powerful impact on demand for a product.

C10-Shortage of a product increase demand.

C11-Promotions, discounts, and redemption enhance sales and demand for a product.

D-How To Launch A New Product?

D1-Persuade the sales force that it is a good product.

D2-Convince trade outlets that it is worth to invest in the new product.

D3-Make the new product available first in retail and later at wholesale outlets.

D4-Ensure strong coverage and distribution in targeted trade channels.

D5-Create outstanding visibility in key outlets. Secure leadership @ POP and erect massive floor display to create high awareness.

D6-Launch intensive TVs Commercials to create-off take and excitement in the market.

E-How to increase demand for a product known to consumers?

Use The Following Schemes To Increasing Demand For A Brand Known To Consumers:

EI-On Pack Promotion

a-Use on-pack promotion on a brand known to consumers to boost its sales.

b-Whenever you want to bring new users to the brand, provide lots of on-pack promotions. This action increases sales and makes consumers augment their purchase of the brand.

c-On-pack promotion is created to reward frequent users. It increases trial and brings new users to the brand.

d- On seasonal occasions, On-pack promotions can be used to block competitors at key WTO's and increases sales.

The above schemes must be implemented with great follow up to achieve high success and productive results.

EII-Getting Rebate

a)-Rebate is used as periodical discounts on famous occasions and seasonality. The aim is to reward users of a brand and to bring new users as well as generating revenue for both trade and the company.

b)-Rebate can also be used to block competitors on occasions and social events. This tactic scheme has been used greatly by FMCG's multinationals.

c)-Rebate can drive more sales volume such as offering free goods on buying a larger quantity would increase distribution and load wholesalers to push the brand down trade.

d)-Rebate is used as extra special discounts to drive more volume. It is used as an offer to wholesalers to achieve the annual targets.

EIII-Run Trade Drive

a)-Run trade drive to widen distribution drive and expand coverage by offering free goods to groceries on buying the brand and displaying it.
Use Key wholesalers WTO's to push the scheme down trade.

b)-Use trade drive as a seeding operation to expand coverage offering free goods or gifts for groceries who buy for the first time the brands of the company, stocking and displaying them. On this drive assign merchandisers or sale-force to display the products on the grocery outlets. Because this is the first time, merchandisers can take advantage of and select the best locations for the products in the grocery outlets.

c)-Offer trade drive to retail channels of WTO's in the form of a discount of extra volume 20%-25% on the pack of the brand to attract new users for the brand. Shoppers and consumers once enter WTO's browse to find offers they are interested in.

Use clear and visible tags so promoted packs can be easily seen by shoppers and consumers.

d)- Give trade drive to WTO's wholesalers with high stock to push their stocks down trade outlets which are not covered by the company main distributor. Thus, increasing distribution, coverage, and reducing the cost of coverage and distribution.

EIV-Provide A Redeem Scheme

a)-Consumers buying redeemed brands are asked to collect brand wrappers and take them to the nearest authorized outlets to redeem and get valuable gifts.

b)-The scheme must be announced through media to create high awareness in the market. Posters and leaflets should be printed to announce the scheme in targeted outlets. The strategy of the scheme is to bring higher and more users for the brands.

c)-Stocking wholesalers and key WTO's will block competitors and win cash liquidity in the market.

d)-Redeem scheme is an important tool for driving high sales, expand coverage, distribution, bringing new users to the brands on the redeem scheme and generate massive sales volume.

EV-BrandSupply Shortage

a)-When a known brand is diminished, the demand for the brand increases, and consequently the price is also incremented. It is known that if the supply of a brand is low, demand goes up for the brand.

b)-Consumers seeking their favorite brand, if it is not available will pay more to get the brand. thus, trade outlets are willing to pay more to get the brand on their shelves and warehouses. It is vital for the success of the outlet is to provide consumers with their inquiries. Do not maintain the scarcity of a brand to increase the price to profit greatly. This has a negative impact as consumers may give up using the brand and buy competitors' brands.

c)-key outlets with a large stock of scarcity brands, increase their margin by increasing the price of the brands which are not available across retail outlets. They took advantage of the scarcity of popular brands in the market and struck a huge profit.

d)-The strategy of increasing the price vs prevailing competitor's price in the market has a negative impact as consumers may develop the idea that the outlet has high prices across all items and as a result, may abandon shopping in the store. For this, it is important to do price analysis every week.
The least favorable outcome for key accounts is to run out of stock of popular brands. A consumer who visits an outlet two times and does not find his/her favorite brand available may change the outlet and select another store for shopping.

EVI-Use TV Commercial

a)-Companies spend a huge amount of money on commercial advertising to increase awareness, market shares, and get their brands connected with customers.

b)-Commercial advertising is essential to generate
sales, enhance off-take, and help retail outlets to
liquidate their stock.

c)-Brands without advertising face slow off-take, poor
awareness. Trade outlets avoid to stock them in large
quantities.

d)-Companies increase commercial TV's number of
spots to support trade, enhance awareness, influence
consumers to increase their purchase, and shoppers
to try and use the brand.

e)-Advertising enhances trade confidence in the
brand and encourages them to increase their
investment in the company's brands.

References

1- Seven Marketing Tips To Create A Demand For Your New Products
https://www.forbes.com/sites/sujanpatel/2016/.../create-a-demand-for-a-new-product/October 22,2016

2- The Six Secrets Of Demand Creation – Fast Company
 https://www.fastcompany.com/1777201/six-secrets-demand-creation Sep 6,2011

3- On Pack Promotions Are Excellent Give Ways To Encourage More Off Taking.
https://www.theodmgroup.com/on-pack-promotions/
Nov 13, 2017

4-5 Way to Maximize Your On-Pack Promotion
https://www.puca.com/5-ways-maximise-on-pack-promotion

5- How to Discount in Retail - https://blog.vendhq.com › Retail Tips & Trends

6-7 Ways to Use Discount Without Hurting You Brand - https://hollerwp.com/discount-without-hurting-your-brand

7- Reward Redemption Behavior in Retail Loyalty Scheme –
https://onlinelibrary.wiley.com/doi/pdf/10.1111/j1467-8551.2008.00561.x

8- Why Scarcity Marketing Doesn't Work For Every Brand-blog.
motivemetrics.com/why-scarcity-marketing-doesn't-work-for-every-brand

9- The Scarcity Principle: How 8 Brands Created High Demandhttps://blog.hubspot.com/marketing/the-scarcity-principle May 10, 2017

10- How do commercial and non-commercial advertisements differ?
 https://www.quora.com/How-do-commercial-and-non-commercial-advertisements dif.

11- What is the Importance of Commercial Advertising?
 https://bizfluent.com › Marketing

12- Why in Store Visibility Matter and How to Improve it – Wiser Retail
https://blog.wiser.com/store-visibility-matters-improve

13- In Store Visibility Program – Visual Merchandising, Visibility Share
www.retail-scan.com/visibility-impact-assessment.html

14- 14 Proven Strategy to Increase Sales of Your Product – Brian Tracy
https://www.briantracy.com/.../sales.../proven-strategies-to-increase-sales-of-your-prod.

15- Forecast and Plan Your Sales – Info entrepreneurs
www.infoentrepreneurs.org/en/guides/forecast-and-plan-your-sales

16- What Sells for FMCG – Business Line
https://premium.thehindubusinessline.com/portfolio/what...fmcg/article8516585.ece

Marketing Mix Of 4P's & 3P's Covers The Following Topics (A-C).

A-The Industrial Model Of The Marketing Mix 4P's
Product
Price
Place
Promotion

B-Summary Of The Industrial Model **Of The Marketing Mix 4P's**

C-The Service Model **Of The Marketing Mix 3P's**
People
Process
Physical Evidence

What Is The Marketing Mix Of 4P's + 3P's?

An organization reaches great success and achieves outstanding results by implementing effectively the marketing mix of 4P's and 3P's. However, to achieve targets and perfect outputs, it is important to possess the skill, resources, knowledge, and the ability to utilize and use efficiently the marketing mix, product, price, place, and promotion + People, process, and physical evidence. Those 7 elements of the marketing mix must work together smoothly as one unit to achieve great revenue and productive results with a profit regarded by investors as promising to achieve high growth, a bright future, and advancement for the company.

A-The Industrial Model Of 4P's.

Product

For a product to be successful and demanded by consumers, it has to have uninterrupted demand in the market with a good reputation and have desirable qualities.

Companies spend massive money to develop, improve, innovate to introduce good quality products, and stay competitive in the market. Those companies bear a huge amount of money on communicating and creating excitement, awareness, and build customers' confidence for their products in the market.

A demand for a product in the market depends on how much money the product invest in publicity, visibility, and knowingness.

Companies pay a large amount of money on building an image for their products through visibility, promotions, advertising,
sampling, and social media marketing.

A Product has to Have A B C D E F G H Characteristics To Achieve Success & Sustain Growth:

A-It should have a stimulating use for consumers and possess the quality and reliability to do what is expected from it and satisfy the required needs.

B-It must have a reasonable, affordable, and competitive price that has value for money paid for users to buy it.

C-It ought to have a name and be reached easily to consumers and shoppers to create awareness and generate revenue and profit.

D-A product needs to be visible at the point of purchase to be seen by consumers and shoppers. It must use commercial TV's and social media to reach consumers, shoppers, and customers.

E-A product should possess an attractive packaging with declared messages and graphics on its packaging to impress shoppers and generate sales and growth

F-A product must be made of good materials, color, and attractive features to build a name for itself, and possess an image in the market.

G-It must have offer different pack sizes and variants to consumers and shoppers.

H-It is strongly recommended that a product should have a warranty. A product should offer a return policy after sales to customers.

According to Philp Khotler, ten entities can be marketed as a product such as:

- Goods
- Services
- Experience
- Events
- Person
- Places
- Properties
- Organization
- Information
- Idea

Source: Philip Khotler the free encyclopedia

Price

1- **The business organization must make sure that ithas priced its product correctly and competitively.**

2- **The price structure has to make sure that all elements of the price structure have been examined to ensure that the price issued has secured a return on investment ROI for trade and the company.**

3- **The price is put on a product. In return, receives value or money for the merchandise and the services it offered to the market.**

4- **The company can increases, decrease, or adjust the price of its product to compete effectively in the market.**

5- **Prices should be reviewed every week to stay competitive in the market.**

6- **It is extremely important to understand the pricing strategy of the competitors to be able to develop a superior pricing strategy against competitors.**

7- **Since price generates revenue, the business should make sure that its running cost is efficient to be able to compete and produce profit for the business.**

8- **The company should secure that all cost elements in the price structure such as distributor margin, best price to trade, and price to retail outlets have been developed with full efficiency and competitively.**

9- **It is crucial to keep checking competitors' prices on a daily or weekly basis to make sure that the set price is correct and conform to current prices in the market.**

10- **Some companies are forced to lower their prices to stay competitive in the market.**

11- **Many companies delist a number of their products or services in the market because of low profitability.**

They justify their action to have more focus on profitable brands with a high margin and to manage financial resources more effectively.

12- **As a price strategy, when you increase the price of some items offer gifts items or extra volume on them.** Most consumers do not remember the old prices and only focus on the promotional offer. **This is important to avoid losing customers. Provide incentives for consumers to buy the product after the price increase. Consumers** forget the old price **and only focus on the promotion of the product when they made their purchase. Design your pricing strategy based on higher revenue and reasonable gross profit.**

13- Some **companies who are facing problems in the market and are unable to achieve annual targets they** use tactical sales schemes **to help them achieve their targets.
Those plans of action such as volume sales drive, redemption scheme, discount payment term on loyalty, offering attractive volume discounts for key traders, on-pack promotion, bundled offers.**

14- **Those companies exercise the mentioned tactical schemes to avoid lowering their prices.
Some companies offer** 2% **or more on the invoice for key wholesale outlets who** buy large **quantities and bring their trucks for loading at the company's warehouses.**

15- **Check competitive prices across trade channels preferably on a weekly bases to stay competitive in the market and to learn if competitors launched new activates.**

16- **Retailers use the following formula to determine their markup price:**

For example, if the average unit cost is $12 **and the desired markup is** 30% **then the price is set at** $ 17. **The calculation is as follows:**
$12/0.7 = US $17

Place

The place is a spot where you can sell your products. A spot can be a hypermarket, supermarket, a large grocery, small grocery, perfumery, pharmacy, wholesalers, and other spots in urban and rural markets. The Trade Channels Are an Example Of a place where consumers and shoppers buy their needs from them.

Promotion.

1- Promotion is a powerful method to attract consumers and shoppers to try a product. Promotion is called the fourth element of the industrial model of the marketing mix. It is an important tool for driving sales up. Companies use promotions to generate higher sales to achieve their targets, build brand loyalty, enhance awareness, create excitement in the marketplace, and build trade and customers confidence in their brands.

2- Most shoppers and consumers when visiting outlets search for products with promotion. They look for simple but popular promotions on the package such as a 20% extra volume or 25% discount on the price, and on-pack promotion with a gift banded on the product.

An example of some promotions is reflected in the below table.

NAME OF THE PROMOTION	DESCRIPTION OF THE PROMOTION
Sampling	Give away the sample of a product.
Coupons	Offer to save on buying a product.
Rebates	The refund is paid on part of the purchase.
Price on Package	20% extra volume or 25% discount on the price.
Premiums	Incentives are given away as free goods (FOC) on buying a product.

Use the above promotions to drive sales up. Selecting promotion depends on the objectives of the sales strategy.

NAME OF THE PROMOTION	DESCRIPTION OF THE PROMOTION
Advertising	Influences consumer & shoppers to buy the product or try it if it is new.
Rewards, Coupon	Attracts tread outlets to buy more of the product. Thus block competitors.
Cash Refund	Creates volume drive by the scheme.
Royalty	Loyal consumers are rewarded due to their loyalty to the brand.
Incentive on attaining target	Customers get gifts at the end of specific time upon achieving their Target.

Use the above promotions to drive sales up. Selecting promotion depends on the objectives of the sales strategy.

NAME OF THE PROMOTION	DESCRIPTION OF THE PROMOTION
Volume drive.	<u>Stock</u> wholesalers, Key outlets, to win cash liquidity in the market. Block competitors.
Visibility contracts	<u>Give</u> a brand greater shelf space or equal to its market share.
Buyback guarantees	<u>Promote</u> a brand in TV advertising and social media
Provide free goods	<u>Drive</u> a brand to consumers by making it available and visible in key outlets.
Contest advertising	<u>Grant</u> a brand wider coverage, and distribution.

Use the above promotions to drive sales up. Selecting promotion depends on the objectives of the sales strategy

B-The Industrial Model Of The Marketing Mix Of 4P's-Summary

Product	**What is the product you want to sell?**
Price	**At what price the product is to be sold?**
Place	**Where consumers can find the product?**
Promotion	**How do consumers know about the product?**

C-The Service Model Of The Marketing Mix Of 3P's.

People

1- **The employees of the company are highly important for the success of the company's marketing and business. The marketing and selling of its products depend on the skill, qualifications, and professionalism of its employees. The company's employees are the ones who meet customers, negotiate with them, and deliver the service. They are highly important for the company image and to achieve its growth year on year.**

2- **When you visit an organization or a business firm to do a potential business with them, your first** impression **on the organization is** its people**. The outcome of your visit positive or negative, in most cases depends on how you were** being treated by **the organization's employees and their attitude.**

3- **In order to ensure healthy business and profit sustainability, it is vital and important to** hire smart **qualified professional people who understand the market and have the** ability & know-how **to execute and deliver superior service to winning trade outlets** WTO's **and win in the market.**

4- **Companies around the world make sure to introduce the right strategy** to train **and develop their employees' skills to run tasks such as customer service, copywriters, deprogrammers, and sales representatives to achieve a productive meeting with customers. Companies** win **in the market because of its professional people who make the right decision in a critical situation.**

5- **Review sales** force-targets **every week to ensure compliance with given targets. This action plan will allow the business to take** corrective **action on time in case of deviation from targets.**

6- Sales-force targets should be reasonable, achievable supported with sufficient resources to ensure positive results, encourage sales-force to work hard to achieve set sales targets, coverage, distribution, and growth.

7- Developing sales-force skills should be reviewed and be updated all the time. Employees should possess full knowledge of the company's products and have the skill to sell them. Customers are heavily influenced by salespeople who have the know-how to introduce and sell the product to them

8- The ability to influence customers to close the deal and make a purchase is a great skill. Make sure that the sales force has developed the skills, including negotiation skills required to influence customers to purchase the company's products. Run training workshops to educate and increase sales-force selling skills, communication, and know-how.

9- The company should develop its sales-force to the stage of professionalism with great knowledge. You could have superior products better than your competitors, however, without the right and professional people to sell it you would not be able to reach the right customers and have effective coverage and distribution to sell your products. This is a fact-based experience.

What Qualification Should FMCG's Salesman Have?

1- Has to have a sense of urgency to respond to WTO's inquires.

2- Has to be an influencer and a good communicator to achieve sales targets.

3- Has to have the qualification and know-how of the task.

4- Has to have the skill required to do the job effectively.

5- Has to have the ability to deliver superior service to clients based on the win-win outcome.

6- Has to be smart and intelligent to establish a productive relationship with WTO's.

7- Has to have a good attitude and friendly appearance.

8- Has to be neat, clean, and dress smartly.

9- Has to have a driving license.

10- Has to be healthy, hard-working, and fit for the job.

11- Has to be loyal and dedicated to the task.

Process

1- When you order a meal in a MacDonald drive-through restaurant, you get your order mostly in less than 5 minutes. This process creates customers' satisfaction because it is quick and fast.

2- The process of loading, unloading, invoicing, delivery of customers' orders have to be quick, cost-efficient, and fast. The business needs to deliver successful customer satisfaction, minimize the running cost of the business, and element the frustration of the customers.

3- It is essentially important for the company to make sure that its system and the process is cost-effective, quick, and friendly to customers and the environment.

4- **Customers get frustrated when the** process is slow **and time taking. It is costly for customers because they lose business when they face out of stock due to a slow process.**

5- **Companies** fail **customers and lose sales and growth if their** processing **system is slow and frustrated. The slow process has a tremendous impact on every function of the company.**

6- **The aim is to develop the operating system and the skill of the employees across all the departments of the company to achieve efficiency and stay competitive in the market.**

Physical Evidence

I-**It is well known that the packaging of a product reflects mostly the quality of the product and the company image. Accordingly, a product needs to look neat, attractive, and possess good packaging to attract customers. Information on the product's packaging of the ingredients must be clear and easy to understand by consumers and shoppers.**

II-**good packaging of a product draws the attention of shoppers and consumers. Thus, companies make sure that the packaging of their products** is appealing **to shoppers.** Poor **packaging is not good for the product. Customers may not pick up the product because of its slummy packaging that gives a negative impression on the product itself.**

III-**It is vital to make sure that** the packaging **of the new product is appealing to customers before launching it into the market. This can be done** by testing the packaging before launching the product.
The company can test **the product and get feedback on the packaging from the target market. Seeking help from packaging** designers **and experts would ensure the success of the product in the market and minimize the failure.**

IV- **On food items, it is extremely important that packaging must be safe to** minimize **the deterioration and contamination of the food. Packaging must also be friendly to the environment.**

V- With good feedbacks from customers on the packaging, companies would be able to reduce the risk of launching unsuccessful products with poor packaging to markets.

VI- Resources allocated for launching a brand can be directed effectively and used efficiently to accomplish a good presentation of the product to the market successfully.

VII- What is important is to make the packaging of the product neat, attractive, and friendly to the environment. You should bear in mind that even small improvements in the outlook of a product packaging such as the label or shape of a bottle of the product may increases sales and profit significantly.

VIII-It is recommended to have a complete check on the buying process in terms of everything that the customer sees from the first moment of contact with your products to the end step of purchasing the product.

IX- What is important is to develop the habit of thinking continually about how the packaging of your brand or product is positioned in the hearts and minds of consumers, and customers against competitors' brands. This could be realized by checking constantly on feedback from the market on how shoppers see the packaging of your brands versus competitors.

X- The packaging is very important for the success of the product. It has to attract customers to pick up the product. Also, salespeople who are selling the product must look neat and professional in every respect. They both reflect the corporate image. It is recommended that sales-force uniforms should be professional, neat, reflecting the company's likeness and image.

References

1- Marketing Mix Definition – 4Ps & 7Ps of the Marketing Mix
marketingmix.co.uk
2- Marketing Mix – What is it? Definition, Example, and More
https://www.kbmanage.com/concept/marketing-mix
3- What Is Meant by a Marketing Mix? – The Balance
https://www.thebalance.com › Small Business › Marketing › Marketing Glossary
4- What is a product? Definition and meaning – Business Dictionary.com
www.businessdictionary.com/definition/product.html
5- What is a product-Product Definition - Define a product - Marketing 91
https://www.marketing91.com › MARKETING BASICS
6- What is a price? definition and meaning – BusinessDictionary.com
www.businessdictionary.com/definition/price.html
7- Price/economics/Britannic.com
https://www.britannica.com/topic/price-economics
8- 6 Different Pricing Strategies: Which Is Right For Your Business?
https://quickbooks.intuit.com/.../pricing-strategy/6-different-pricing-strategies-which-i
9- Price Markup Calculator, Calculate selling price with mark up percentage.
everydaycalculation.com
10- Marketing Mix/ Place in Four 4Ps – Cleverism
https://www.cleverism.com/place-four-ps-marketing-mix/
11- Place – Marketing Mix Distribution Strategy – The Marketing Mix
marketingmix.co.uk/place
12- Place in the Marketing Mix: Definition & Concept – Video & Lesson
https://study.com/academy/.../place-in-the-marketing-mix-definition-lesson-quiz.html
13- Marketing Place – Marketing Teacher
ww.marketingteacher.com/marketing-place/
14- Explain the Marketing Promotional Tools in Details
ww.businessstudynotes.com/marketing/.../explain-the-marketing-promotional-tools
15- Organizations & People – MNP LLP
ww.mnp.ca/en/consulting/organization-and-people
16- People and Organization – PwC
ttps://www.pwc.com/ca/en/services/consulting/people-and-organization.html17-
People/EFQM
ww.efqm.org/efqm-model/efqm-model-in-action/people
18- 10 Tips for Effective Employees Performance Reviews
ttps://www.businessnewsdaily.com/5760-write-good-performance-review.htm
19- McDonald's Drive-Thru: One Minute Service or Free Food
time.com › Everyday Money › Food & Drink
20- physical Evidence – Marketing Mix – Marketing Teacher
www.marketingteacher.com/physical-evidence-marketing-mix/
21- Marketing Mix Physical Evidence – Marketing Mix
marketingmix.co.uk/marketing-mix-physical-evidence
22- The Important of Attractive Packaging
https://www.parekhplast.com/blog/the-importance-of-attractive-packaging

<u>Customer Marketing Covers The Following Important Topics:</u>

A-What Is Customer Marketing?

B-How To Grow Current Customer?

C-Segmenting Consumers Market

Demographic Segmentation
Geographic Segmentation
Psychographic Segmentation
Behavioral Segmentation

D-Customer Marketing Guideline & Strategy

What Do Shoppers & Consumers Want?
What Do Customers Want?
What Do Companies WANT?

E-How To Increase Important Customer Profitability?

F-How To Develop In-Store Activities?

The objective of Customer Marketing is to focus on current Key Winning Trade Outlets WTO's where the company brands are achieving excellent results and have the potential to grow further. Those outlets contribute more than 80% of the company's business. Hence, customer marketing management will ensure better and greater customer service, more promotions, strong leadership visibility at the POP with excellent floor displays at key locations across WTO's.
The aim is to achieve cost-effective operations with superior and outstanding results for the business and WTO's. The rest of the market will be covered by key wholesale outlets WTO's supported by lots of promotion and sales drives activities under the close supervision of the company's distributor sales force and the business customer development management. To secure a successful output, it is vital to action the below procedures:

1- Set **The Goal For The Winning Trade Outlets (WTO's).**

2- Pass **The Goal To The** WTO's.

3- Get WTO's **Commitment To Achieve The Goal**

4-Action **The Goal** And Achieve It.

B-How To Grow Current WTO's?

To achieve successful business growth with WTO's, it is vital to apply the following steps with great follow up:

1- Understand key winning trade outlets (WTO's-wholesale channel) in detail in terms of strengths and weaknesses and how they can be used to push the company's brands across trade channels in urban and rural markets to achieve growth for them and the business.

2- Determine your market position in WTO's against competitors to drive the right promotion and in-store activities to generate higher sales and volume.

3- Decide your financial marketing budget against the set target.
Take corrective actions in case of deviation from the growth plan, coverage, and distribution.

4- The sales force must report competitors' activities in key outlets daily to encounter them accordingly.

5- Ensure company's brands' shelf space in (WTO's hyper and supermarkets) equal to market share or greater according to visibility contracts. Use POS materials and massive visibility, as well as an attractive TV screen, shows in key winning trade outlets to communicate the brand message to shoppers and consumers. Make certain that a relationship with WTO,s is based on a win-win outlet comes.

6- Provides WTO's with tailor-made promotional activities. give support to liquidate slow-moving brands by packs and by variants. Such action would encourage WTO's to invest more in the company brands.

C-Segmenting Consumer Market

Segmenting Consumer Markets allows the company to set up the strategy for pricing its products, launching new products, innovations, promotional activities, and targeting consumers by areas, regions, and cities. See clarifications stated as below:

1- Demographic
Age, gender, family size, income, education, occupation, religion, race, generation.

2- Geographic
Nations, regions, states, countries, cities, areas.

3- Psychographic
Social class, lifestyle, spending habits, values, personality, interests, hobbies.

4- Behavioral
Knowledge, attitudes, brand loyalty, and rate of usage.

1- Demographic
Demographic segmentation **states that companies collect lots of information on consumers for launching a product, and to maximize productive coverage and distribution. The objective is to** understand the market in terms **of ethnicity, family size, income, education, race, age, gender, and religion to target markets more accurately and productively.**

2- Geographic

Geographic is understanding the market in terms of Nations, States, Regions, Countries, and Cities. This assists to target markets more accurately with effective coverage and distribution. Action the below steps vigorously:

a) Divide **the city or regional large** territory into small areas and zones **to develop an accurate journey cycle for the sales-force and to give sufficient** focus **to each entity by salesforce routes to markets and territory management.**

b)-**Provide customers with different services and directions according to their needs, by brands and capacity for growth.**

c)-Assign **an efficient journey cycle to the sales force group to cover divided zones effectively and monitor them accordingly to take corrective action in case of deviation. Support should be given as per area sales and potential growth.**

d)-**The** aim **is to cover** all **winning customers** WTO's **and reach their outlets effectively. Companies apply this strategy to serve** a wide **geographic customer base on a local or regional territory and to be able to manage available resources more effectively.**

3- Pyscohgrphic

a)-**Psychographic is addressing consumers' lifestyle which is a manner of living that reflects the person's values and attitudes and social class of people having the same level of economy and education. For this, it is vital to develop a decorous design for a brand or a product with** attractive **packaging to secure a strong off-take.**

b)-**It is important to understand consumers** and **shoppers deeply to influence their decision purchase process.**

This know-how can be obtained from research companies who study consumers and shoppers' behavior in great detail.

c)-Segmentation helps companies to develop, comprehend, and understand consumers in detail in terms of what they like and what they do not like. consumers have different personality traits, opinions, interests, values, attitudes, and lifestyles.

4- Behavioral

a)-Behavioral segmentation is screening the market from different appearances or aspects. Information obtained from the market on consumers' knowledge, attitudes, brand loyalty, and rate of usage is analyzed carefully. The strategy is based on understanding market feedback on consumers purchasing behavior.

b)-Data has revealed that consumers have a diverse perception of a product based on their knowledge, appearance, backgrounds, attitudes toward the product. Companies categorize consumers into classes to provide the right product and service to them.

Customer Marketing Guideline And Strategy

A-What do shoppers & consumers want?

a1-Value For Money

a2-Brand Experience

a3-Shopping Convenience

B-What do outlets want?

b1-Sales Growth

b2-Increase Profit

b3-Offer Brand Tailor Solution And Lots Of Promotions

C-What do companies want?

C1-Gain Higher Market Shares

c2-Increase Profit

c3-Achieve Growth On ROI

E-How to increase the WTO's sales & profitability?

Run below activities every month:

I- Drive in-store activities on fast-moving pack sizes.

II- Provide gifts on spending a certain amount of goods purchased from the outlets participated in the schemes.

III- Create outstanding visibility on POP and massive floor displays.

IV- Ensure 100% availability of fast-moving pack sizes and variants.

V- Provide in-store Sampling And Sales events.

VI- Ensure prestigious customer service based on a win-win relationship.

VII Create excitement by offering WTO's sales events **to attract more foot traffic, consumers, and shoppers to their outlets.**

VIII-Ensure the right assortment at **the correct location of the shelf space. Establish** constant **leadership** at the POP.

IX-Improve **company system sales processing. Accelerate the process of taking orders from customers such as invoicing, loading, and unloading. Deliver customers' orders on time and according to their orders**

F-How to develop in-store activities?

a)-**Increase coverage & distribution by offering free goods** FOC. **Go for higher coverage and distribution using sales drive activities and** seeding operations.

b)-**Incentivize key wholesalers to push the company's brands down trade by giving them a certain quantity of the company's brands on achieving set targets. Run the sales drive in rural and urban markets covered by wholesalers.**

c)-**Provide incentives to salesforce based on a target of a** 20% **increase in sales and the number of outlets covered.**

d)-**Ensure effective and efficient** use **of Trade Marketing Investment** TMI. **Spent should be efficient and according to the allocated budget.**

e)-**Secure productive Sales** & **Operation Planning** S&OP **across all functions. Meeting of** S&OP **Management should** review **the process and agreed with numbers, timing, and delivery every week.**

References

1- **Customer Marketing Strategies That Help Keep Our Client Happy**
https://www.wordstream.com/blog/ws/2016/04/19/customer-marketing-strategies

2-**The Guide to Customer Marketing-Customer Success Software**
https://www.gainsight.com/2017/06/02/guide-customer-marketing 3-
What is Customer Marketing-Search Engine Land
https://searchengineland.com/what-is-customer-marketing-271009

4-**Learning From Unilever's Insights Engine: tapping into "People.**
https://www.bordbia.ie/learningsfromunilever'sinsightsenginetappingintopeople insi

5-**Product Visibility on the Shelf With Eye-Tracking – Cool Tool**
https://cooltool.com/market-product-visibility-on-the-shelf?item=168744311

6- **The importance of the store environment – Marketing Science**
marketing-sciences.com/importance-store-environment-work-harder/

7-**10 Steps For Successfully Launching a New Product or Service**
https://www.fastcompany.com/.../10-steps-successfully-launching-new-product-or-ser

8-**Why It's crucial to understand the shopper's in-store behavior**...https://WWW -retailcustomerexperience.com.

9-**Customer Marketing Articles & Best Practices – Marketo**
https://blog.marketo.com/category/customer-marketing

10-**18 Very Effective Methods to Get Quality Customer Feedback – OptiMonk**
https://www.optimonk.com/.../15-ways-e-commerce-websites-get-customer-feedback/

11-**8 Brilliant Way to Sell Excess Stock Fast – Edge Insights Blog**
blog.edgepri.com/6-brilliant-ways-sell-excess-stock-fast.

12- **Basic Explanation of Demographic Segmentation With Example**
https://marketingwit.com/demographic-segmentation

13-**A Simplified Explanation of Geographic Segmentation With Examples**
 https://marketingwit.com/geographic-segmentation

14- **Psychographic Segmentation Definition – Marketing Dictionary – MBA**
https://www.mbaskool.com › Concepts › Marketing and Strategy.

15-**MarketingTheory. Behavioral Segmentation-SlideShare.**
https://www.slideshare.net/monikaba5/marketing-theory-behavioural-segmentation

16-**Operational Marketing Strategies**
https://yourbusiness.azcentral.com › Small Business Basics › **Operating a Business**

Visibility & Merchandising Covers The Following Topics (A-J)

A-Job To Be Done On A Daily Basis @ Important Trade Outlets WTO's

B-The Power Of Visibility

C-The Power Of Sampling

D-The Power Of Outstanding Displays

E-Selecting A Shelf Space For A new Product Recently Launched

F-Selling Shelf Space

G-Shelf Space Inventory

H-Share Of Shelf

I-V isibility & Merchandising Guideline And Strategy

J-Visibility & Merchandising Strategy

<u>A-Job To Be Done Daily At WTO's</u>

1- **Brands' share of the shelf should be according to their market shares.**

2- **The brands have to be displayed on the shelves' space assigned for the categories.**

3- **Leading brands should get more facing at the POP and be merchandised daily by both the owners of the brands and the outlets**

4- **Packs with high margin should get more facing. This important for both outlets and the company.**

5- **Leading brands should have floor displays in prominent locations for higher awareness and off-take.**

6- **Place large packs at the lower shelves for better handling and shelves management.**

7- **Provide a proper cooling system to keep the products at convenient cooling temperatures at delivery trucks and in the outlets.**

8- **Secure 100% availability of fast-moving SKU's**

B-The Power Of Visibility And Merchandising

I-**Your products must be seen and easily accessed by consumers and shoppers whether in large or small outlets to be picked up and purchased. For this, multinationals and prominent local companies construct massive displays at the POP and make outstanding floor displays in key winning outlets WTO's to impress and influence shoppers and consumers to buy their displayed brands.**

II-**When a product is on the right outlet, on the correct shelf with the attractive and proper POS materials, it is highly expected that sales, the profit of the product go up. The product has to be seen easily by consumers and shoppers to buy it and achieve sales growth.**

III)-**Establish outstanding visibility for key brands or newly launched products at the point of purchase POP across key WTO's to enhance awareness, sales, and publicity.**

IV- **To win with WTO's, It is advisable as a sense of urgency that you ensure delivery of their orders on time and as per their purchase orders. For slow-moving packs help WTO's to liquidate them by providing stimulus to consumers to accelerate their liquidation. It is recommended to take back stock which is not moving or expired. This would establish trust with the trade and encourage WTO's to invest more in the company's brands. This is the responsibility of the sales force to follow up with trade outlets.**

V- **Every week, coordinate a meeting between the Customer Development CD team, Customer Marketing, Marketing, and Supply Chain SC to analyze weekly feedback from the market on the company's business results and performance vs competitors.**
Proper action must be taken in case of deviation from the company sales strategy. The aim is to ensure vigorous successful follow up and stay competitive in the market.

C-The power of sampling

The power of sampling is huge and extremely important in bringing new users to the brand. It is important to follow the below recommendation:

a)-Erect an attractive display in key outlets and prominent locations for the product which is going to be sampled. People who are going to perform sampling must dress neatly and should have perfect know-how of the product that they are planning to sample.

b)-Sampling on–the–spot provides shoppers with close detail on the product. It allows shoppers to ask, examine, and get information on the product. It is critical and mandatory that the sampler has sufficient and needed knowledge on the product.

c)-Use special offer on pricing, such as buy 2 get 1 free on purchasing the sampled product. Give a gift to incentivize shoppers to buy the product. If the product is food, let them taste the product.

d)-Utilize shelf-talkers, leaflets, danglers to communicate the advantages of using the product and its value to shoppers.

e)-Display a large banner next to the sampler announcing sales offers.

f)-Sampling should be as close as possible to cash registers. For this, get permission from the outlet to put up sampling stands in the vicinity of the main flow of shoppers in the outlet. This is important to enhance awareness and increase exposure to sampling so shoppers can see the sampling activity before leaving the outlet.

g)-The sampling stand should be decorated with POSM and leaflets, danglers, the flag of the product, and have an attractive image or photos of the sampled product.

<u>D-The power of outstanding POP and floor displays</u>

a)-An outstanding POP and floor displays across key trade outlets WTO's creates excitement, builds a brand image for displayed brands. it enhances awareness, increases off-take, trial, and influences shoppers to buy displayed products.

b)-It also blocks competitors and has a very powerful influence on turning shoppers into buyers.

c)-When you make a visibility contract with key winning outlets WTO's give more shelf space to fast-moving packs with a higher margin. Make sure to invest and use every centimeter of your shelf visibility contracts effectively. Ensure constant sufficient stock to secure 100% availability to increase sales, block competitors, generate profit, and to secure full shelf space all the time for your products.

d)-Prominent local and multinational companies are displaying their products in such a way to stimulate interest and entice consumers to increase their usage and shoppers to make a purchase. Those companies buy shelf space and make contracts with key important trade outlets to secure high visibility for their brands.

e)-It is recommended to make displays especially for newly launched brands with a promotional offer on them close or near the front of the store or before reaching the cash registers. This is important to remind shoppers to try and pick up the brand.

f)-Creating this Point Of Purchase POP position in the vicinity of cash registers is intended to attract the consumers' and shoppers' attention as they are making their final purchase.

A-For a new product recently launched, It is important to put the product on the right shelf space assigned for the category of the same products.

B-It is highly recommended to place the new product near or next to the right of brands with known names on shelves so shoppers can see it.

C- The new product should have an attractive colorful point of purchase materials POPM with a clear message to capture the attention of shoppers. Erect a prestigious floor display for the new product close to the cash register for more awareness, trial, and off-take.

D)-Make sure that the stock of the newly launched product is 100% available across all K. winning outlets WTO's.

E-Customer Case Fill On-Time CCFOT is the flow of stock from the company's distributors to trade outlets. It should ensure 100% availability of the new product recently launched at the point of purchase POP in the WTO's any time those outlets are visited.

F-Promotion on the new recently launched product on the shelf or special stands must be communicated to consumers and shoppers with bright colorful tags and clear messages.

F-Selling shelf space

a)-Top retail outlets such as hyper, supermarkets, large pharmacies, and mega perfumeries get high valuable income from selling shelf space, and floor displays to top local and multinational companies. Some well-known hyper and supermarkets chains charge a fee for the listing and registering the products in their system.
As a result, when top outlets construct and design their outlets, they make sure that every centimeter of their outlet's shelf space is regarded as scarce resources and must be managed with great effectiveness.

b)-The impact of visibility on the sales of displayed products is huge and massive. It has given those outlets the power to charge a high price for their shelf space

c)-The objective of retail outlets is to maximize their financial gain from selling shelf space. However, this depends on the success of the retail outlet in the market.
The outlet has to attract high foot traffic by offering promotions once every weak, so it can put a lucrative price on its shelf space. For this, It is strongly recommended that retail outlets construct shelf space in a very attractive and spacious design to capture the attention of shoppers and secure attractive visibility for displayed brands.

d)-The traders have to generate profit from selling shelf space to improve their revenue and ensure growth for their business.

e)-Space management is a good source of revenue for WTO's if it is managed and organized with great efficaciousness. Rationalizing share of space, fixing the shelf attractively, erecting gondolas at key positions, and ensuring floor displays at prominent locations generate higher profit for the outlet.

f)-Bear in mind that the objective of space management is to manage shelf space rationally to secure 100% availability of fast-moving packs and variants every time Winning Trade Outlets WTO's are visited by consumers and shoppers.

g)-Good shelf space management provides an important mechanic for trade outlets to forecast their merchandise needs at the store level. Shelf space management is critical and has to secure assortment with 95% to 100% availability of fast-moving packs and variants to achieve sales growth and guarantees sustainable ROI growth.

h)-Keeping track of fast-moving packs and variants with high margin is vital for generating an accurate forecast and a high return on investment ROI. The management of the stock inventory at the company's warehouses has the responsibility to secure 100% stock of WTO's.

G-How to reduce out of stock cost?

1- Secure an accurate forecast based on feedback from sales date and stock in hand. The forecast should give priorities to the fast-moving brands by important SKU's.

2- Out of a stock is a loss of sales. It is not healthy for both the company and trade outlets. It minimizes growth and reduces foot traffic. As a result, it is important to secure stock and ensure 100% availability 24 hours a day, 7 days a week. Trade outlets and companies are investing in the shelf space stocks expecting100% availability and positive ROI.

3- Companies are buying shelf space to stock them fully, block competitors, and avoid out of stock. from key outlets and look forward to getting high sales and profit. This should be done with outstanding merchandising. Ensure to secure superior delivery on time and reach excellent customer service to achieve higher sales and generate a lucrative profit.

4- Keeping track of the fast-moving packs and variants with a high margin is vital for generating a high return on investment ROI. The management of the stock inventory at the company's warehouses should be alert of the fast-moving SKUs. It has the responsibility to secure 100% of the vital stock of WTO's.

5)-It is very critical for the success of both the company's business and the trade outlets to increase sales and minimize out of stock. Space Management Inventory SMI has to provide the right forecast and provide effective direction to WTO's on how to manage their stock rationally and practically. Constant follow up is the key to success.

H-How To Improve Shelf Space Inventory?

1)-Make sure to secure the inventory of the visibility of fast-moving packs with high margin at POP with 100% availability. Fast-moving packs should have more facing. This is important even in case consumers and clients purchase less during economic hardship. Outstanding visibility builds the brand image, enhance awareness, and generate high sales and profit for both trade outlets and the company. This fact should be communicated clearly to trade outlets.

II)-Improve the efficiency of managing the running cost of inventory to be able to reduce the overall running operation cost of the stock. This is necessary to generate and secure profit and growth.

III)-Establish assortment efficiently on the right shelf to cover fast-moving packs by variants based on 100% availability seven days a week. This has to be agreed with the supply chain in the S&OP weekly management meeting. Ensure strong follow up with solid implementation.

IV)-Provide a mechanic that can help WTO's to reduce the cost of stock lists, optimize inventory, improve shelf availability, and increase sales and margins. Ensure a productive relationship with WTO's to help trade achieve a production forecast. Such support will assist WTO's to improve the inventory running cost and increase their business, generating revenue, and profit

V)-Not having the right product demanded by consumers is a business lost to the outlet. Most consumers abandon visiting the outlets who experience out of stock because it is costly for them to make a trip to the outlet and not find their needs. Most retailers face continuous problems of not having the right inventory at the right time every time their outlets are visited by consumers. This is for sure as a result of poor follow up by salesforce and supply chain. Those retailers repeatedly experience out of stocks or overstocks which is very costly to them. The problem can be confined to vigorous updating the system of inventory on a daily bases and follow up of fast-moving pack sizes by variants to ensure 100% availability.

I- What Is Share Of Shelf?

Share of the shelf is what is the measurement of the brand on the shelf allocated for the category of the brand. Managing share of the shelf by brands according to their market shares is profitable for key WTO's as they are investing in those brands and the available shelve at their outlets. As a policy, the company should always seek to establish a share of the shelf for its brands, and categories in winning WTO's equal to the share of the market or greater than the share of the market in case the opportunity allows. This is important and vital for brand building, visibility, greater off-take, and sustainable growth and profit. Most multinationals and prominent local companies make shelf contracts with K. winning trade outlets WTO's to ensure better shelf space for their brands according to market shares or greater in some cases. WTO's avoid as much as possible to invest in brands with low market shares due to poor ROI on them.

Visibility And Merchandising Guideline Strategy

Trade Channel	% Of Coverage	Merchandised By Salesforce Team	Merchandised By merchandisers' Team
Hypermarket	100%	Nill	Yes
S/Market A S/Market B	100%	Nill	Yes
Pharmacy Perfumery	50%	Yes	Nil
Large Grocery	50%	Yes	Nil

The above visibility and merchandising guideline strategy for trade channels were designed to ensure focus, growth, and to minimize running cost.

References

1- Visibility, Display & Merchandising/ Shop ability
shop-ability.com.au/services/activation/category.../visibility-display-merchandising/
2- The Benefits of product Sampling: Why you should do it/ Factory 360_
https://factory360.com/the-benefits-of-product-sampling-why-you-should-do-it
3- How to Use Samples to Promote Your Product/Inc.com_
https://www.inc.com/guides/.../how-to-use-samples-to-promote-your-product.html
4- Retail Merchandiser APP/ Brand Visibility Tracking/ Branding App
newtel.in/merchandising.htm
5- Sore visibility: Is Your Merchandising Attractive – Simplified
simplifield.com/retail-tomorrow/enhance-store-visibility/
6- Visual Merchandising: How to Display Products in Your Stores_
https://fitsmallbusiness.com/visual-merchandising-guide/
7- The hidden war over grocery shelf space-Vox_
https://www.vox.com/2016/11/22/.../grocery-store-slotting-fees-slotting-allowances
8- How to Get You Product on the Shelf of Any Store – Reply_
https://www.repsly.com/blog/consumer-goods/how-to-get-your-product-on-the-shelf
9-A study on shelf space allocation and management – Science Direct_
https://www.sciencedirect.com/science/article/pii/S0925527398001340
10-FMCG Distribution-Improve FMCG Inventory Management With CRM
https://www.kapturecrm.com/.../how-inefficient-fmcg-distribution-slows-down-your-b.
11-Relationship between inventory management and uncertain demand.
https://www.sciencedirect.com/science/article/pii/S2351978917300963

<u>Principle 6, Routs To Markets Covers The Following Topics (A-J)</u>

A-**What Is Route To Market?**

B-**Coverage Strategy**

C-**How To Select Important Winning Trade Outlets - WTO's?**

D-**Frequency Of Coverage Of** WTO's

E-**What Is Bill Productivity** BP?

F-**What Is Line Per Productive Call** LPPC?

G-**How To Secure 90% Of** BP&LPPC?

H-**How To Build Growth For Your Product?**

I-**Segmenting** WTO's **By Their Needs?**

J-**How To Design Coverage Strategy For** WTO?.

A-What Is Route To Market?

Selecting the right Route To Market (RTM) to achieve excellent coverage and distribution and to produce outstanding customer service requires great skill and deep knowledge of consumer markets. Every company aims to design and set up a productive RTM strategy coverage and distribution to reach its customers before competitors with an efficient running cost.

Good RTM contributes to the success of the company's pricing strategy of its products, launching new products, chosen promotional activities for individual outlets, and targeting consumers by areas, regions, and cities with the right product and pack size to satisfy their needs and offendable to their budget. RTM must possess deep knowledge and understanding of the market's demographic, and geographic, to design the right Journey Cycle JC for the company's salesforce by areas, by markets to achieve great profitable results.

The objective is to understand the market in terms of ethnicity, family size, income, education, race, age, gender, and religion to target markets more accurately and productively and to develop successful RTM.

Every retail van salesman will only carry in his van the right brand by pack size. This is important to achieve productive and successful coverage.

B-Market Structure-Example

Below is an example of the market structure where Fast Moving Consumer Goods FMCG's are sold which is self-explanatory. Diagram-1

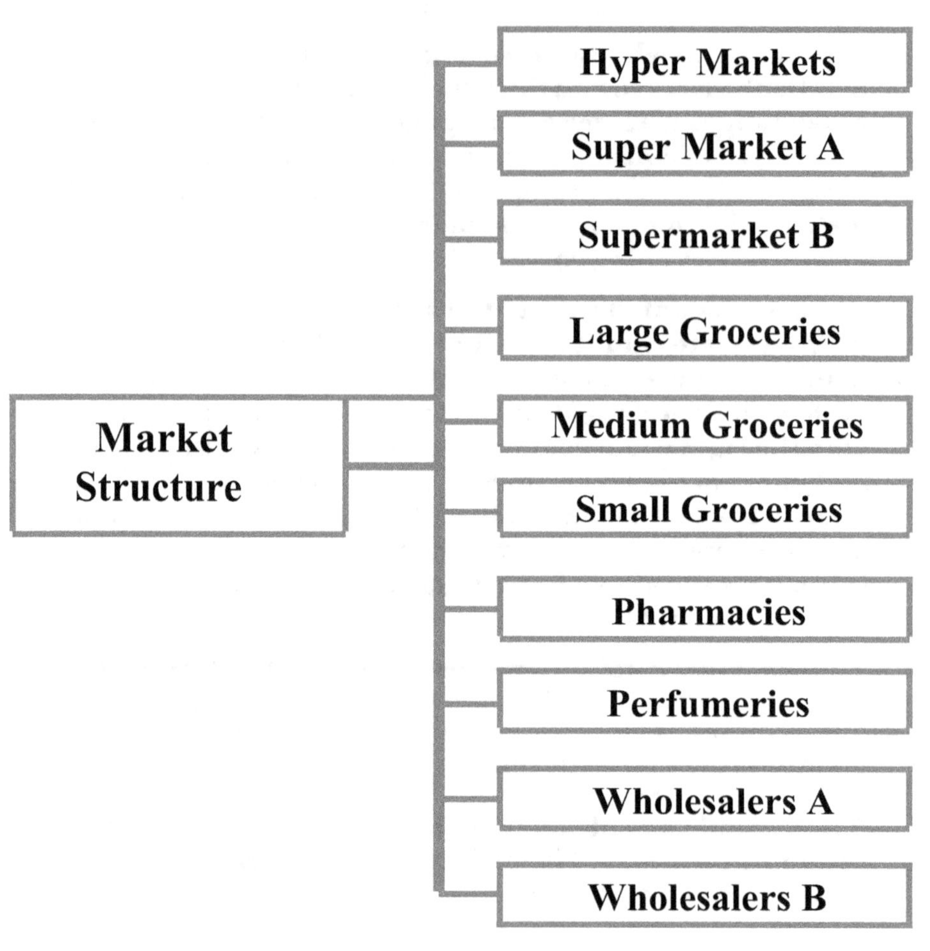

Diagram-1

C-Coverage Strategy-Example.

The coverage strategy of the company will be divided into three coverage strategies:

I- Direct Coverage by The Company's Warehouses.

II- Direct Coverage by the company's Retail Van Salesmen.

III- Indirect Coverage by the key Wholesalers.

Hypermarkets, Supermarkets, and top key wholesalers would be connected with the company warehouses through an internet computer network system to supply them with the needed stock. The objective is to provide those top trade channels directly with the important SKU's (Stock Keeping Unit) and secure 100% availability of fast-moving SKUs for those outlets. The mechanic is that all sales transactions of the company products by pack size and variants from those outlets would be recorded and monitored by the company warehouses stock system and would be replaced based on the agreed stock level substitutability between the company and the outlets. See below diagram-2

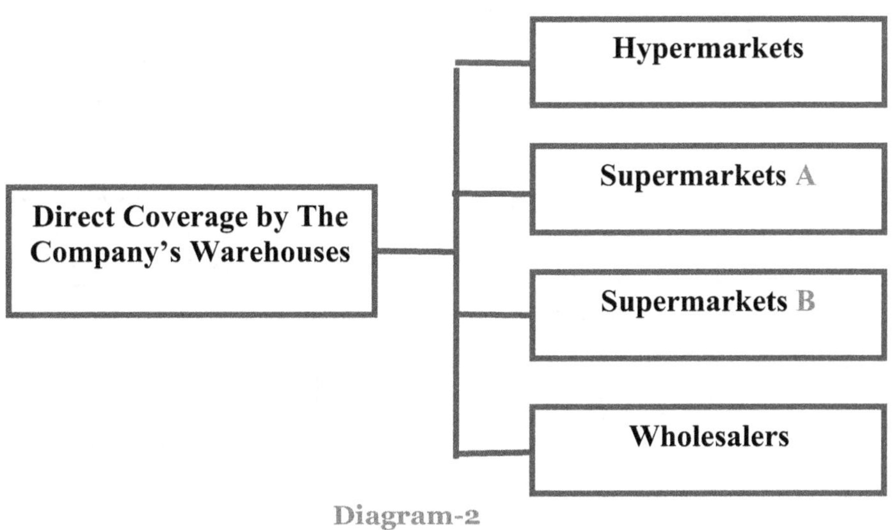

Diagram-2

All the above trade channels stated in diagram-2 are designated as Winning Trade Outlets WTO. The coverage strategy must provide them with outstanding focus and first-class customer service.

Retail van salesmen will be using sales technology handheld computers connected with the company's warehouse main computer system to monitor and to have full control over the outlet's trade sales transactions, credit limit, stock in hand, stock sold, and pending invoices if any that have not been paid or settled.

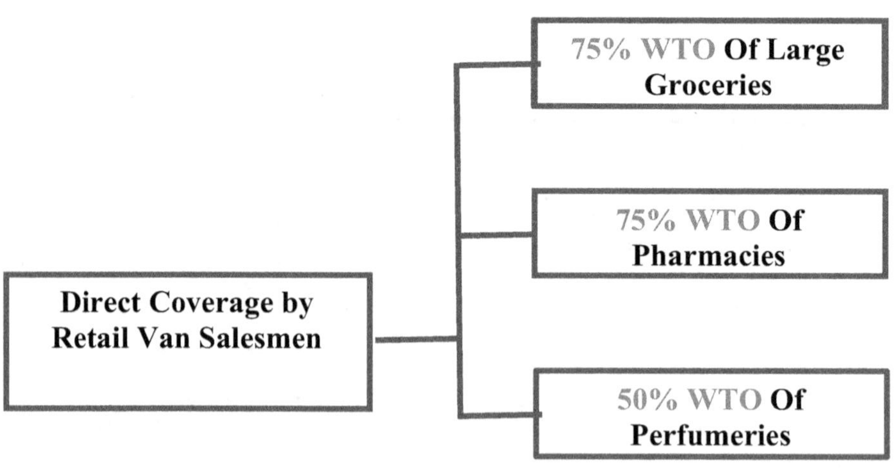

Diagram-3

III-Indirect Coverage by Wholesalers Under the Supervision of The Company dedicated supervisors. Every month special schemes will be offered to those outlets buying from designated wholesalers. Diagram-4

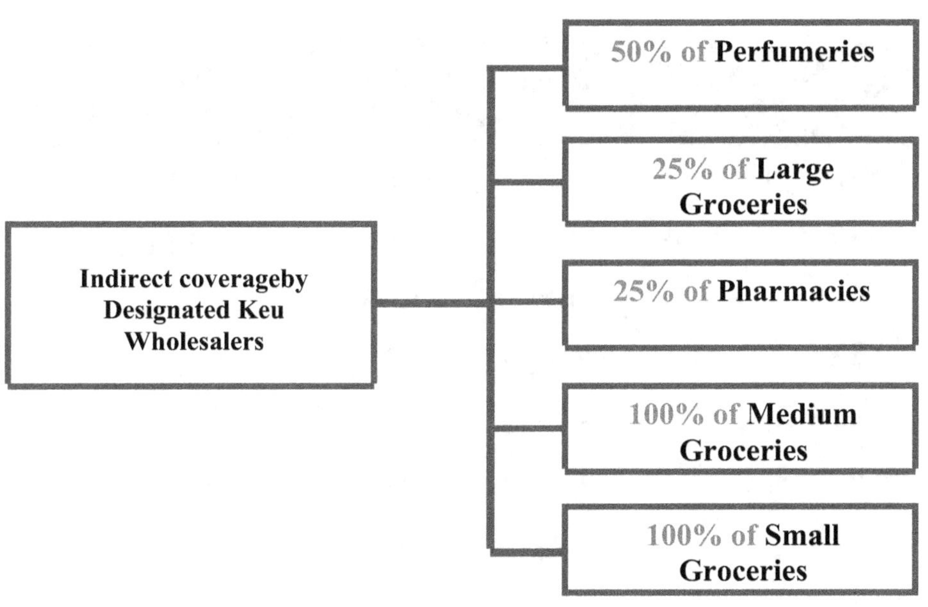

Diagram-4

D-Sales Strategy Coverage

In the below example, the coverage strategy is designed to cover only Winning Trade Outlets WTO's see below table 1 where the company's brands are growing and have the potential to grow further. The coverage strategy by trade channels is reflected in the below table. The objective of the sales strategy is to provide those WTO's by trade channels with a maximum focus of coverage and first-class customer service. WTO's selected from every trade channel will receive priorities in terms of promotions, delivery of placed orders on time, and provide them with outstanding customer service and beautiful merchandising. The other retail trade outlets will be covered by WTO's Wholesalers under the dedicated supervisors of the company customer development team. They will be provided with great sales schemes and other incentives to cover them successfully.

Channel	Universe	Coverage Strategy	# Of Covered Winning Trade Outlets WTO's
Hypermarket	540	100%	540
Supermarkets A	754	100%	754
Supermarkets B	982	100%	982
Large Grocery.	16,238	75%	12,179
Pharmacy	4327	75%	968
Perfumery	3265	50%	2,185
Wholesalers	532	100%	532
Total	26,638	73%	18,140

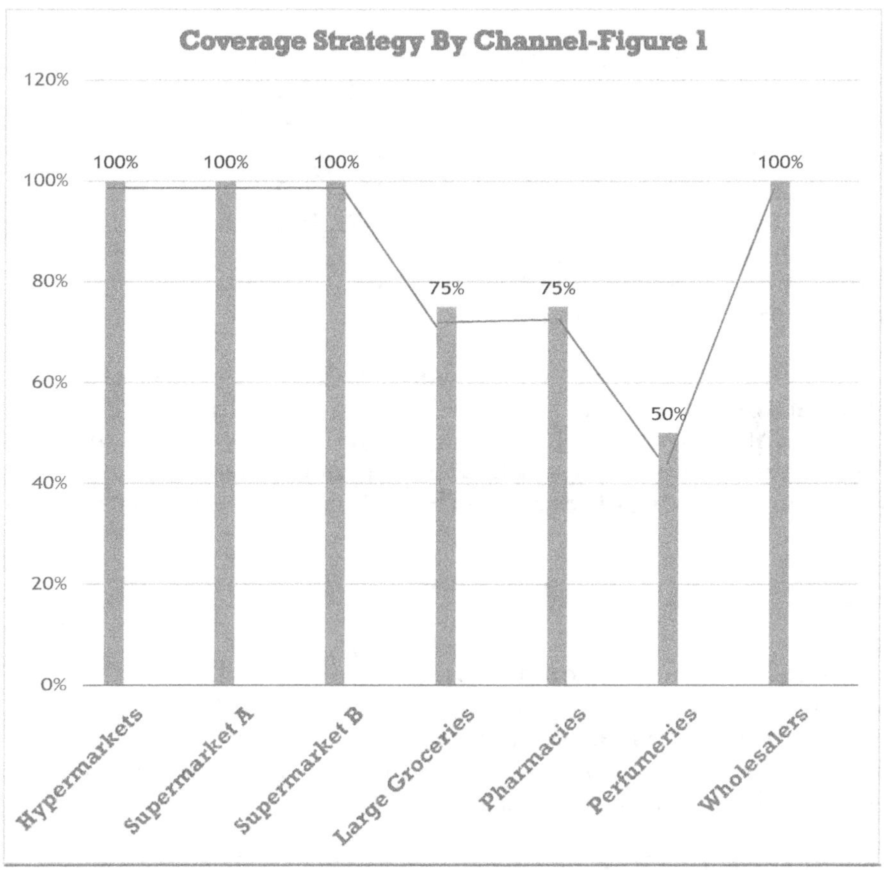

E-How to achieve effective direct coverage?

a)-Divide the city or regional large territory into small areas and zones to develop accurate journey cycle JC for the sales-force and to give sufficient focus to each entity by brand, by pack size, and by promotion.

b)-Select Winning Trade Outlets WTO's by trade channel in each area to provide them with effective and proper services and directions according to their needs, by brands, by pack size, by variants, and capacity for growth.

c)-Assign an efficient Journey Cycle JC to the salesforce to match each area's needs and to monitor them effectively and to take corrective action in case of deviation from set target and growth. <u>Each retail van salesman should load into his van only brands by pack size and by variants to use the space of his van efficiently and to avoid carrying products that have no demands in his JC.</u>
Support and other promotions should only be given as per area sales and potential growth.

d)-The aim is to reach WTO by area and by channel before competitors. As a sense of urgency, it is extremely important to provide all winning trade outlets WTO's with fast-moving brands by pack size and variants as needed and secure outstanding focus and first-class customer service.

F-How to select Winning Trade Outlets -WTO's

I- Do a SWOT analysis on potential important outlets WTO's by trade channel to select the right important outlets you intend to cover. It is important to get reliably detailed information on the important trade outlets for every channel before selecting important outlets.

II- The objective is to preserve and grow existing important trade outlets WTO's and securing profitable new important outlets.
Your coverage strategy must fit your capability, resources, and market insight.

III-To ensures return on investment and achieves sustainable profitable growth, you must fully understand the market and the important trade outlets in which you operate. Strong follow up with a sense of urgency is key to success.

IV-Strengthen your focus on sales, and distribution to maximize old and new and old revenue. Achieve profitability by focusing vigorously on important fast-moving SKUs with a high margin. It is highly important to secure 100% availability of strong brands.

V-Get everyone in product management, marketing, sales, supply chain, customer service, and distributors, partners, aligned together, understand the strategy to maximize sales, profit, and customer service for important outlets.

VI-Determine the optimal level of spending for each function such as marketing, sales promotions, events, and customer service for each key important outlet.

G-What is Numeric & Weighted coverage?

I- Numeric Coverage

Assuming that the total number of outlets in your area which you want to cover is 100 outlets. As a result, the universe in the area is 100 outlets. If you decide to put your product into 20 outlets. In this case, your numeric coverage is 20/100 that is 20%. However, if you decide to cover all 100 outlets to achieve wider distribution, your numeric coverage distribution is 100%.

II- Weighted Coverage
In case you decided to cover only Winning Trade outlets WTO's across trade channel and according to the sales strategy mentioned earlier where your sales to those outlets contribute more than 80% of your sales categories, your coverage is weighted distribution. You decided to cover WTO's across the trade channel to achieve a higher focus on availability, visibility, and reduce the overall running cost of coverage and distribution.

If the company strategy is to cover all outlets in the universe regardless of their contribution to the business, then the coverage is called numeric distribution.
However, if your strategy is to cover important outlets, such as winning trade outlets WTOs, in this case, your coverage is called weighted distribution.
Covering WTO's is regarded as Weighted Distribution.

When you launch a brand, make sure your brand is available 100% in WTO's with outstanding visibility at Point Of Purchase POP with superior floor displays decorated with attractive POSM to achieve maximum focus, influence shoppers and consumers, and to provide higher customer service.
Putting your newly launched brand in winning trade outlets WTOs will allow you to get quick feedback from the market as you have full control over winning trade outlets WTO's. Numeric Distribution is based on Universal Coverage. However, Weighted Distribution is based on selected outlets WTO's which contribute higher % to your business.

H-Sales strategy Coverage Continues

Assuming that currently, the company has 169 SKU's (Stock Keeping Units) for sales in its warehouse. To ensure 100% availability of the company's fast-moving SKU's, Hypermarket's Supermarkets and key important wholesalers will be connected to the company's warehouses through modem and internet systems. The objective is to replace the company's products by pack size and variants once products are sold by the hyper and supermarkets. An agreement will be signed with both hypermarkets and supermarkets to determine the stock level that should be replaced immediately by the company once the stock level is down or out of stock. The company SKUs are taken from the following categories reflected in the below tables.

Note: Coverage of other WTO by channel will be carried out by retail van salesmen.

Table - 2

I-Home And Personal Care Categories

Skin Care	Fabric Wash
Personal Care	Home Care
Hair Care	Toilet Tissues
Oral Care	Paper Products

Talcum	House Cleaners
Deodorants	Shoe Care
Cosmetics	
Perfume	

Table - 3

II- Process Foods Categories

Ice Creams	Juices
Baker Products	Coffee
Cereals	Bottles Waters
Chocolates	Vegetables
Snack Food	Sugar
Soft Drinks	Rice
Tea	Dairy Products
Health Beverages	Confectionary

I-The frequency of the coverage of the sales strategy of WTO's is as follows:

I- **The frequency of the coverage of the sales strategy of the WTO's is daily.**
The objective of the sales strategy is to focus on covering WTO's during set working days whether they are hyper, supermarkets, pharmacy, perfumery, large grocery, or key wholesalers. It is important to establish a constant connection, superior customer service and strong follow up with WTO's inquiries to be able to serve them effectively.

II- **WTO's urgent orders will be delivered during the weekends as well. For the rest of the market, the coverage will be given to wholesalers who will push the company's brands down trade and to medium and small groceries as well as other outlets in both urban and rural markets using special retail trade drives.**

III- **Wholesalers will be supported with special schemes, like redemptions, distribution drives, and other incentive schemes. The company's customer development management and dedicated distributors sales supervisors will be monitoring sales from wholesales to trade daily. You must bear in mind that follows up is key to success.**

IV- **Daily feedback from the market on competitors' pricing strategy, sales drive schemes and in-store activates should be reported by salesforce and merchandisers daily.**

J-What is effective coverage?

Salesforce covering winning trade outlets WTO's must ensure 100% availability of fast-moving packs and their related variants. 100% availability is only valid when targeted products by SKU's are available any time WTO's (Winning Trade Outlets) are visited.
The leadership of key brands at POP should be outstanding all the time with POP materials to enhance awareness and build up the brand image to influence shoppers and

consumers to purchase the displayed brands. See the below table # 4 which demonstrates the required task for effective coverage strategy. See the below table:

Table–4

Required Task	Task To Be Done
Availability	100% every time the outlet is visited
Visibility	Leadership @ POP every time the outlets is visited
Delivery of orders	Every day and on time
Number of visits	Every day
Sales drivers	Monthly – offering attractive promotions and other offers
In-store activity	Offering gives away gifts and others on a monthly basis.
Sampling	Weekly offering attractive gifts & free goods

K-Company's branches – This is just an example.

The company has seven branches to cover the entire territory of the country. The detail on the management structure of the branches is as follows. The below table # 5 is just an example:

Table – 5

Branch	Number of salesmen	Number of sales supervisors	Deputy branch manager	Branch manager
	20	3	1	1
B	18	3	1	1
C	15	2	1	1
D	12	2	1	1
E	11	2	0	1
F	14	2	1	1
G	10	2	0	1
Total	100	16	5	7

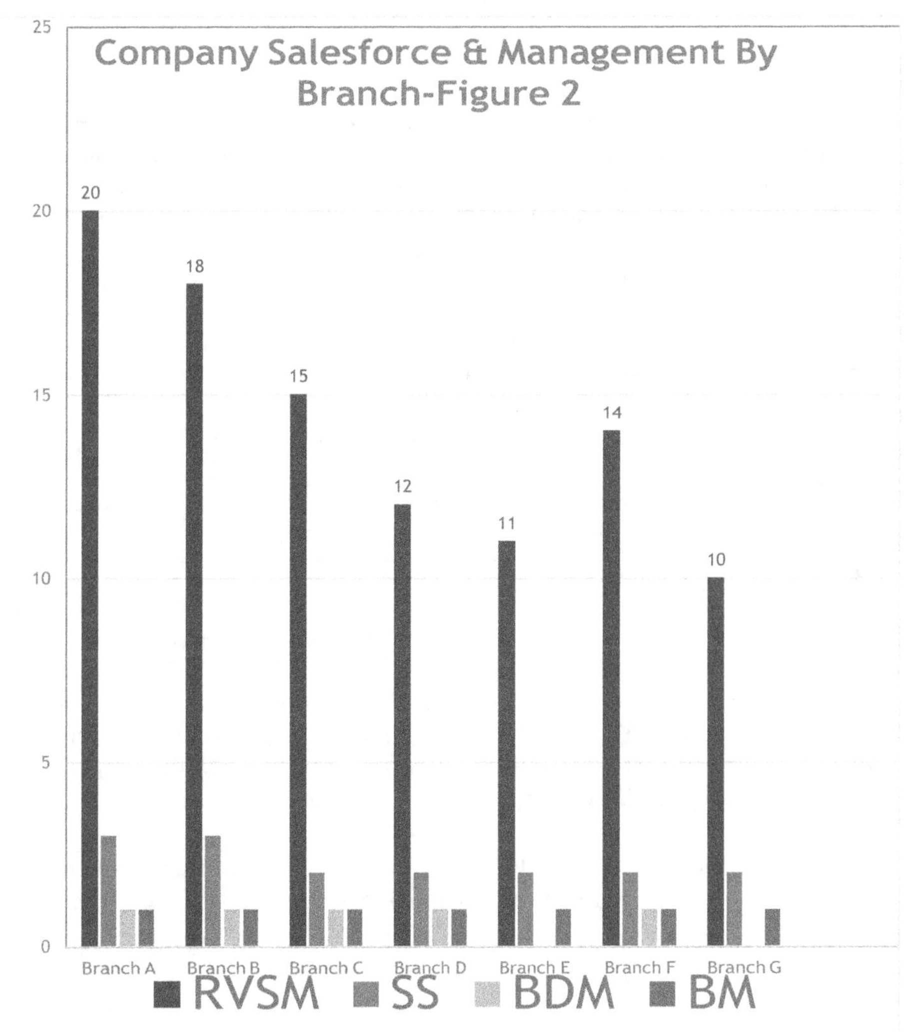

RVSM=Retail Van Sales Man
SS=Sales Supervisor
BDM=Branch Deputy Manager
BM=Branch Manager

<u>Retail van salesmen are the backbone of the salesforce.</u>

L-Branch Scorecards - KPI

Every branch must have to have a scorecard to measure its performance against set targets. Such measurement is called Key Performance Indicator or KPI which provides the branch and the company a clear way to evaluate the branch performance results against set targets. KPI gives the branch a set of facts and feedback to compare results against given targets and allow the branch to take corrective action in case deviation from set targets is observed.

Below is an example of KPI for the branch manager, Deputy branch manager, sales supervisors, and retail van salesman. The KPI will be issued every month against given set targets.

Table # 6 is an example of the Branch Manager monthly Scorecard KPI.

	Monthly Value Target	% Achieved	CCFOT Target	% Achieved
Branch Manager	$ 1,000,0000		100%	

The branch value target = The branch monthly and annual value target has to be achieved by the branch manager and his deputy. Achieving the branch target is their responsibility. It is a task that must be done by the branch manager and his deputy.

CCFOT = Customer Case Fill On Time. CCFOT. The branch manager must ensure 100% availability of fast-moving SKUs at WTO every time the outlets are visited.

M-Sales Supervisors Scorecard – KPI Example

Name:
Branch:
Position: Sales Supervisor

	Monthly Value Target	OSA	CCFOT	RVST
Target	**$ 200,000**	**100%**	**100%**	**100%**
Achieved				

Job To Be Done

I-Value target = **Monthly and annual value targets must be achieved.**

II-OSA = **On Shelf Availability of fast-moving SKUs must be secured and achieved for WTO.**

III-CCFOT = **Customer Case Fill On-Time CCFOT of WTO by trade channel must be achieved. The availability of the fast-moving SKUs must be confirmed every time those WTO are visited.**

IV-RVST = **Retail Van Salesman Target. Sales supervisor has the responsibility to follow up with retail van salesmen targets and make sure that retail van salesmen achieve their targets.**

<u>Retail van salesman Scorecard - KPI</u>

Name:
Branch:
Position: Retail Van Salesman

	Value Target	BP	LPPC	SKU's Sold/ SKU's Loaded
Target	$ 100,000	%100	10	100%
Achieved				

<u>Job Must Be Done</u>

I-Value Target = 100% of **the value target must be achieved by the end of the month.**

II-BP = **The average Bill Productivity** BP **for the month should not be less than** 95%. **The above is just an example.**

III-LPPC = **The average Line Per Productive** LPPC **Call for the month should not be less than** 10.

IV-SKU's Sold÷SKU's loaded = **The average** SKU's **Sold divided by** SKU's **loaded into the van of the retail salesman should not be less than** 100%

<u>O-Setting targets for retail van salesman
Bill Productivity BP</u>

In the below example, the retail van salesman has to achieve
4 targets to ensure productive healthy coverage and
distribution. The targets should be delivered fully by the end
of the month. It is extremely important to achieve
productive and healthy coverage and distribution to secure
success and sustain growth for the company. The 4 targets
are as follows:

I- **Monthly** value target **must be achieved** 100% **by the end of
the month.**

II- **Monthly Bill Productivity** BP **should be** 100%. **The daily
number of visits to the retail salesman is fixed at** 14 **visits
per day.** BP **formula is as follows:**

$$BP = \frac{Number\ of\ Invoices}{Number\ of\ visits}$$

III-**Average Line Per Productive Call** LPPC **should not be less
than** 10.

$$LPPC = \frac{SKU'\,sold}{Number\ of\ Invoices}$$

IV-**Average monthly sold** SKU's **by the end of the month
divided by the** SKU's **loaded into the retail van salesman
should not be less than** 100%.

<u>Setting targets for retail van salesman-Bill Productivity BP Continues.</u>

I- Retail van salesman value target.
At the beginning of every month, the retail van salesman will be given a monthly value target based on his Journey Cycle JC which is based on brands demand by pack size fit for the territory coverage capacity, and previous month's performance. The target will only be given to him after settling his precedent month targets. The value target must be achieved by 100%

II- Bill Productivity (BP)
The retail van salesman should be given BP target to be able to monitor his effective coverage and daily performance during the month. Further detail on BP is as follows:
a- Bill Productivity BP is the number of invoices divided by the number of visits. It increases when the number of invoices escalates against the number of visits.

b- Since the coverage is only on WTO's which are known to the company in terms of inquiries, strength, and weaknesses, the number of visits is set at a minimum of 14 visits per day per salesman.

c- Consequently, retail van salesman has to achieve at least 14 invoices per day against constant 14 visits to achieve 100% Bill Productivity. The number of visits is limited to 14 visits per day which are not difficult to achieve. The goal is to give more time for the salesman to spend with the targeted outlets to achieve healthy sales.

d- For achieving more than 100% bill productivity, the retail salesmen will get a bonus at the end of the month.

$$BP = \frac{Number\ of\ Invoices}{Number\ of\ visits}$$

See the below example on retail van salesman performance which reflects BP increases when the number of invoices obtained grows up.

Below is an example of Bill Productivity BP for retail van salesman performance for a week Sunday-Thursday.

Number of invoices obtained per day	S 12	M 11	T 13	W 12	Th 13
The number of visits is constant	14	14	14	14	14
$BP = \dfrac{Number\ of\ Invoices}{Number\ of\ visits}$	87%	79%	93%	87%	93%

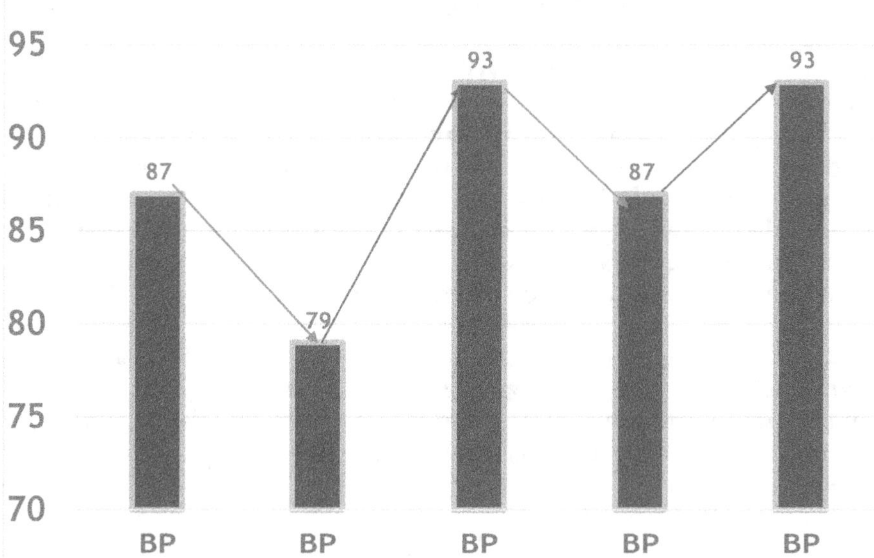

The above graph shows that as the number of invoices increases, BP grows up. Higher BP enhances coverage, distribution, brands build-up, sales, and profit. The average BP for the week and the month per salesman should not be less than 100% for the retail salesman to be productive and achieve his/her target smoothly.

<u>Q-Line Per Productive Call LPPC</u>

III- What is Line Per Productive Call – LPPC?
<u>LPPC</u> **is measuring retail van salesman coverage and distribution. It is equivalent to the number of Stock Keeping Unit** SKUs **sold divided by the number of** invoices.
In principle, **more** SKUs **sold per invoice increase distribution and result in achieving healthy sales.**

$$LPPC = \frac{SKU' \, sold}{Number \, of \, sales \, Invoices}$$

As mentioned earlier **the** total **company's** SKUs **available for sale are** 169 **SKU's.**
Every retail van salesman will be given a target based **on his Journey Cycle** JC and area of coverage. **The salesman will** only **carry** SKU's **convenient for his** JC. **Outlets buying targeted** SKU's **should be able to sell them and make their margin profit. This is important to achieve healthy sales and avoid selling** SKU's **which cannot be sold by the outlets and later expired in the outlets and at the end must be taken from the outlets which are costly to the company.**

LPPC **is focusing on distribution. Selling more** SKU's **per invoice leads to higher distribution and sales.**
See the below table which indicates that LPPC **increases as the number of** SKUs **are augmented per invoice.**

The below example **shows the retail van salesman Line Per Product Call** LPPC **performance for a week** Sunday-Thursday.

	S 1	M 2	T 3	W 4	Th 5
Number Of SKU's Sold	134	90	126	95	137
Number Of Invoices	12	11	13	12	13
$LPPC = \dfrac{SKU'\,sold}{Number\ of\ sales\ Invoices}$	11	8	9	8	11

The above table shows that selling more SKU's **increase** LPPC**. The above example used the same number of invoices for the retail salesman** BP**. On day** 1**,** LPPC **=11 is the highest because with only** 12 **invoices and** 134 SUK's LPPC IS 11**.** LPPC **augment distribution of the company** SKU's **and thus help to build the brands** SKU's **and reduce the stock cost and running costs of coverage.**

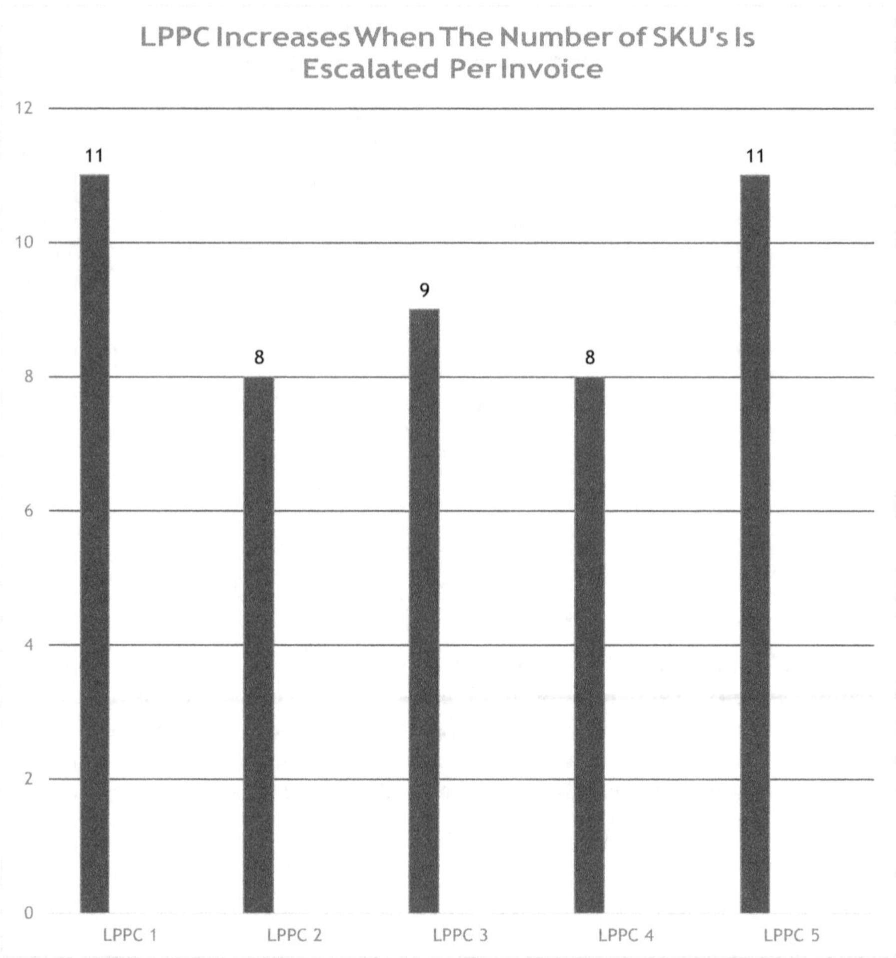

The above figure shows that more SKU's per invoice increases the distribution. Thus, build the business, enhance profit, and return on investment.

The below <u>example</u> is representing a month performance of a
retail van salesman for a month:

	Target	Achieved	% Of Achievement
Monthly Value Target	USD 300,000	USD 276,000	92
BP	100%	97%	97
LPPC	10	9	90
SKU's sold/SKU's Loaded	100%	97	89

The above results are good but not excellent. The retail van salesman has
not been able to achieve the monthly value target and LPPC. Thus, he
should be given support and more guideline to achieve higher results.

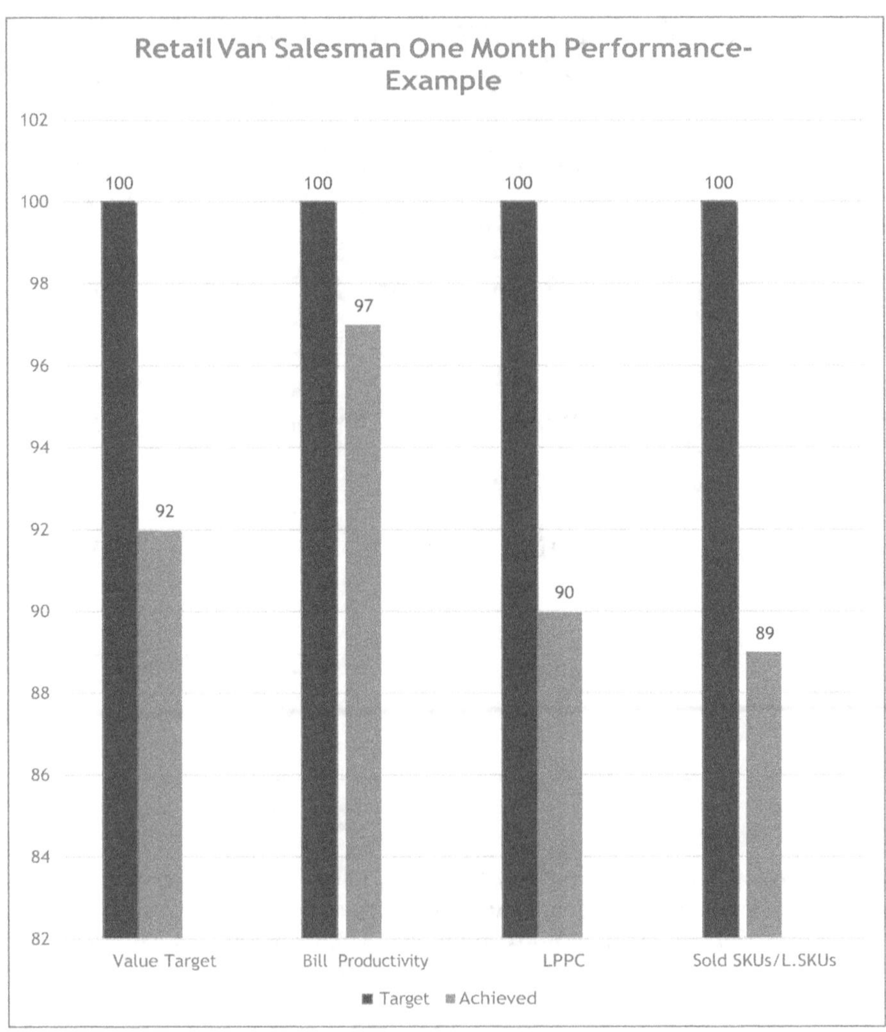

The above figure shows that the retail van salesman is facing a problem with the value target and liquidation of the stock in his van.

R-How to secure 100% outcome For BP& LPPC?

I)-Branches must ensure 100% availability of key SKUs at WTO's to achieve higher sales.

II)-Branches have to create strong off take by establishing leadership at the point of purchase with daily merchandising. It is strongly recommended to erect outstanding floor displays decorated by POP materials

III)- Branches have to assure daily delivery of WTO's orders on time-based on the urgency to avoid out of stock of important and highly demanded SKU's.

IV)-Branches should create a productive relationship with trade based on the win-win outcome.

V)-Branches have to divide WTO's into areas for focus and design effective coverage and distribution.

VI)-Branches should accelerate loading, invoicing, and unloading of WTO's orders.

VII)-Branches should implement with great follow up the promotional schemes offered by customer development management of the company and ask for help and support in case needed.

References

1- **Smarta-Routs to markets**
www.smarta.com/advice/sales-and-marketing/sales/routes-to-market/
2- **Routs - to Market (RTM) - Paramarketing**
paramarketing.com/routes-to-market/
3- **Three Steps for Creating a Successful Route to Market Analysis.**
https://blog.euromonitor.com/.../three-steps-for-creating-a-successful-route-to-market-.
4- **How to choose the right route to market – entrepreneur Handbook**
https://entrepreneurhandbook.co.uk › Marketing
5- **How Is Pick And Pack Distribution Beneficial?-Commercial**
https://www.commercialwarehousing.com/.../how-is-pick-and-pack-distribution-benef.
6- **What is Channel Strategy?-Definition from WhatIs.com**
https://searchitchannel.techtarget.com/definition/channel-strategy
7- **What is Channel Strategy? What Marketers Should Know**
https://blog.hubspot.com/marketing/what-is-channel-strategy
8- **Investor, know thyself: Choose A Stock Category Based On Your Risk**
https://www.investopedia.com/.../investor-know-thyself-choose-stock-category-based
9- **Five habits that make for better supermarket inventory management**
https://www.relexsolutions.com › Blog › Inventory Management

Principle # 7 Covers The Following Topics (A-H):

A-**How To Win With Winning** WTO's**?**

B-**How To Prepare Sales Strategy?**

C-**What Is Share Of Shelf SOS?**

D-**How To Prepare Joint Business Plan JBP?**

E-**How To Develop Growth Strategy For JBP?**

F-**What Is Joint Business Plan Scorecard?**

<u>**A-How To Win With Winning Trade Outlets-WTO's?**</u>

a)-**Provide winning trade outlets** WTO's **with** top **customer service. Assign** dedicated supervisors by areas **to cover** WTO's **to create focus and to follow up with their orders and activities in their outlets. The effective coverage of winning trade outlets** WTO **depends on reaching them at the right time and delivering their orders on time.**

b)-Manage smartly **your brands with** WTO's **by winning the right shelf space at a** POP **for key fast-moving packs with** high margin. **Ensure to run massive floor displays, in-store sales events, promotional activities, sampling, and customer service with top efficiency. Establish a weekly meeting with** WTO **to review their business performance and how to provide support to growing the business.**

c)-**Manage your business in winning trade outlets** with great focus. **Establishing a win-win business relationship is a great success for both the company and Winning Trade Outlets** WTO's **as well.**

d-**Success is achieved when you have continuous** 100% **availability with outstanding visibility at the** POP **for the company's key brands with high margin across winning trade outlets** WTO's. **Achieving constant growth year on year, gaining market shares, covering the right outlets by areas and, operating with** 100% **efficiency on the journey cycles is a great accomplishment. Ensure to establish vigorous follow up to achieve your goal.**

e)-**For focus and effective coverage, divide winning trade outlets** WTO's **by areas and group them by priority, rank them to create an efficient route to the market dedicated to achieving strong coverage and** 100% **availability of fast-moving** packs **with high** margin. **Secure outstanding customer service and superior merchandising.**

f)-Competitors' activities in winning trade outlets WTO's must be reported on the daily market report. To be competitive in the market you must encounter their activities using vigorous schemes. In brief, you have to win the satisfaction of WTO's by matching competitors' offers and in some cases offering greater promotions.

g)-Select Top 10 or more of winning trade outlets WTO's to establish joint business planning JBP with them. The choice should be based on SWOT analysis outcome, measure their financial ability, and strength, position in the market to determine each customer target accurately. JBP targets must be agreed with customers in a written agreement and followed up by both the company and the customers as well.

h)-Assign a special sales force team responsible for developing and covering the top selected 10 winning trade outlets WTO's. The salesforce has to have full knowledge of how to develop the business of the company in those outlets. Their challenge is to follow up and achieve the targets set for WTO's. They should possess the full skill and sense of urgency to respond productively to the needs of their customers, able to handle such large outlets, and have sufficient resources to respond to competitors' challenges.

i)-The salesforce responsible for coverage top 10 customers must be skillful in communication skills to build a win-win relationship with those top important customers. BP, LPPC, ECO should have a score above 95% for those top important customers.

B-How To Prepare Sales Strategy?

a)-The sales strategy has to facilitate growth for Winning Trade Outlets WTO's where the company's brands are doing excellent and have strong potential to grow further. The objective is to maximize revenue and drive down the cost of sales and distribution by focusing on winning trade outlets WTO's growth and building the brand market shares.

b)-The sales strategy has to provide sufficient resources and detail of coverage by priority by areas and by brands to ensure successful outcomes. The strategy has to be aligned with marketing, customer marketing, customer development, supply chain, and finance to coordinate the commercial aspect and manage cost-effectively.

c)-A successful sales strategy is to achieve the following:
Achieve growth for the existing business WTO's.
Acquire new business. Develop new WTO's.
Expand the business with a yearly growth of a target of 12% for example, over the previous year.

d)-The company's brands are measured by its brands' market shares. You gain higher market shares by introducing invocations, sales activities with a constant 100% availability, and strong leadership at POP with attractive POS materials, TV commercials, sampling, and lots of consumer promotions.

e)-Establish network connections with winning trade outlets WTO's and the company warehouses using IT technology with a modem connection to establish 100% availability of fast-moving pack sizes at all times and achieve superior customer service.

<u>C-What is Share Of Shelf (SoS)?</u>

1- **Share Of Shelf** SOS **is the share given to a brand out of the total shelf space area allocated for the category of the brand. For example, if** 20 **meters is the total shelf granted for the category. If brand** A **has** 4 **meters shelf space, the** SOS **of the brand is** 20%.

2- **Higher** SOS at POP **increases sales, strengthen the brand image, influence shoppers to buy the brand, and augment** ROI.

3- **On** national **occasions and** seasonal **events, greater** SOS **block competitors, increase market shares, build the brand image, and reduce the brand out of stock.**

4- **Generally, the share of the shelf should be equal to the market share of the brand. However, most companies seek to have greater** SOS **for their brands to generate higher sales for their brands. Some companies make shelf contracts with key accounts to secure greater shelf space than the brands' market shares.**

<u>D-How To Prepare Joint Business Plan-JBP?</u>

a)-**Select the top 10 or more of** WTO's **to make** JBP **with them. Set a target of** 25% or less **growth over the previous year. Get** WTO's **agreement on the target and ensure collaboration and partnership, by both key winning trade outlets** WTO's **and the company. Drive alignments and action plans designed to achieve set targets and achieve** 25% **growth.** JBP **is about alignment between selected top winning trade outlets** WTO's **and the company.**

b)-**The Joint Business Plan** JBP aims **is to develop the business** WTO's **and the company's. It is about growth and constant** 100% **availability and leadership at a** POP. **It is highly recommended to do a** SWOT **analysis for targeted key winning outlets** WTO's **accounts to get a clear and full picture of their position in the market as well as the**

competitors in their outlets and how to come up with a
vigorous plan to establish leadership in the targeted outlets.

In Brief

I- **Select Top 10 or More of** WTO's **In Growing
Channel.**

II- **Set Targets**

- **Set a growth target by category, for example, at
  25% or Less Agree on Target With** WTO's.
- **Define activity planner by month (Jan-Dec.)**
- **Agree on priority growth by brand by fast-moving
  SKUs with a high margin.**
- **Get financial support.**

III- **Action With Flawless Execution.**

IV- **Monitor and Adapt.**

E-How To Develop Growth Strategy For JBP?

1- **Establish constant leadership at the point of purchase** POP
and ensure full collaboration with customers to grow sales.

2- Create **accurate forecast by brand by pack sizes by variants
and by category for** JBP **top selected** WTO's. **Ensure accurate
forecasts to avoid out of stock or overstock.**

3- Ensure 100% **availability of the fast-moving brand by pack
size with good margin** at every WTO's across all channels.
Secure more facing for packs with high margin.

4- Provide **sufficient support for financial resources. Align
tactical activities with key winning outlets** WTO's.

5- **For** JBP, **targets and growth should be agreed with** WTO'S
**and to get their commitment. Establish followed Up daily,
and in case of deviation, corrective action should be taken to
ensure compliance with agreed targets.**

6- **At the end of the cycle operation, results must be
evaluated against the agreed target to ensure good results for**
JBP.

Sales-force responsible for JBP must work with a sense of urgency 24 Hours to secure 100% availability, ensure leadership visibility at WTO's and secure strong follow up.

F-What Is Joint Business Plan Score Card?

Job To Be Done	KPI	Specifying Individual Role	Setting Review Methods
Set 25% annual target growth for key WTO's on the company's categories	Monitor and achieve 25% annual growth	Customer Development Management	Monthly
Achieve 100% availability of core brands	Get 100% availability every time the outlet is visited.	Sales-force and supply chain delivery system	Daily
Establish leadership and POP, ensure a share of shelf equal to or greater than the share of the market.	Accomplish leadership and POP as set by targets.	Sales-force and merchandisers	Daily
Execute In-market activities as per the agreed activity planner.	Achieve activity planner as set by the activity targets.	Customer Development Management and sales force.	Weekly
Deliver key WTO's orders on time.	Deliver orders of Key WTO's on time.	Supply Chain and sales-force	Daily

References

1- What is market coverage? Definition and meaning_
www.businessdictionary.com/definition/market-coverage.html
2- Successful Market Coverage Strategy-The Path of Retailers_
www.diva-portal.org/smash/get/diva2:4427/FULLTEXT01.pdf
3- What is the difference between the numeric distribution and weighted_
https://www.bayt.com/.../what-is-the-difference-between-the-numeric-distribution-and
4- Numerical and weighted distribution in retail_
https://community.tableau.com/thread/220542
5- 7 Steps To Build A Successful Sales Strategy
https://aliceheiman.com/7-steps-to-build-a-successful-sales-strategy/ 6-
5 Steps To Creating An Effective Sales Strategy
https://www.inc.com/project.../5-steps-to-creating-an-effective-sales-strategy.html
7- What Is Point – Of – Purchase Marketing?
smallbusiness.chron.com › Advertising & Marketing › Marketing
8- Capturing "First Moment of Truth" Understanding Point of Purchase._
www.msi.org/.../capturing-the-first-moment-of-truth-understanding-point-of-purchase
9- Category Optimization – The Partnering Group_
www.thepartneringgroup.com/manufacturer-consulting/.../assortment-optimization/
10- What Is Planogram? Definition from whatIs.com
whatis.techtarget.com/definition/planogram
11- How To Read a Plan-O-Gram – Chorn.com
smallbusiness.chron.com › Advertising & Marketing › Product Plans
12- Point Of Purchase Displays: Benefit and Best Practices For Retailers._
www.merrittgraphics.com/blog?id=123994/point-of-purchase-displays-benefits.
13- What Is On Shelf Availability?
https://www.igi-global.com/dictionary/on-shelf-availability/52714
14- Why On Shelf Availability Is Critical – Supply Chain Brain
www.supplychainbrain.com/nc/.../why-on-shelf-availability-is-critical-for-retailers-1/

8-Shoppers & Consumers Insights
Principle # 8

Principle # 8 Covers The Following Topics (A-H):

A-**Shoppers Insights.**

B- **Understanding The Below Factors To Achieve Growth.**

C-**What Are The Stimulus To Create A Purchase?**

D-**Turning Shoppers Into Buyers.**

E-**How To Turn Shoppers Into Buyers?**

F-**Who Is The Consumer?**

G-**Understanding Consumer Insight**

H-**What Are The End Objectives Of Shoppers/Consumers, Traders, & Brand Owners?**

A-Shoppers Insights

A Shopper enters a store walks around and makes his or her decision at the shelf in the outlet. In the shopping process, people behave differently. Their behavior depends on how they are influenced by the shopping drivers or stimulus which are as follows:

a)-**Promotions.**

b)-**Price discount on buying two items or more.**

c)-**Extra volume 25% more on the large packs.**

d)-**Sampling**

e)-**Rebates offers.**

f)-**Contests offering attractive gifts.**

g)-**Point of purchase leadership and attractive floor displays.**

B-Understand The Below Factors To Achieve Success & Growth.

1)-**The shopping experience**

2)-**Shopping occasions**

3)-**Shoppers behavior-instore reaction**

C-What Are The Stimulus to create a purchase?

a)-**On pack promotion with gifts.**

b)-**Price discount on buying 2 or more items.**

c)-**Extra volume 25% or more on large packs.**

d)-Sampling offering gifts and sponsoring events.

e)-Rebate offers.

f)-Contest offering attractive gifts.

g)-Greater influential visibility at a POP.

g)- Massive display of the product before check out.

D-Shopper Insight-Turning Shoppers Into Buyers.

Shoppers may visit large outlets such as hyper or
a supermarket and leave both of them without buying
anything. The strategy is to influence shoppers not to leave
the visited outlets without purchasing. This can be achieved
by offering them the right shopping drivers mentioned
earlier to turn them into buyers.
Get market feedback on similar activities that you are
planning to introduce as an activity planner for the month or
a quarter. It is vital to make sure that the WTO's have input
in the activity planner to get their commitment and
productive input on the activity.

E-How To Turn Shoppers Into Buyers?

1- An outstanding visibility, merchandising layout
and, leadership at the point of purchase with clear messages
of the product on the shelf influences shoppers to try the
product and may become permanent buyers of the product in
case they like the product.

2- An attractive price off on the product such as buy one get
one free, 25% off or more draw the attention of shoppers to
buy the product.

3- Good advertising strongly increases awareness with high
possibility turns shoppers into buyers.

4- **In store activation and sampling influence shoppers to buy the product especially if there is an offer on the sampled product.**

5- In brief, **the shoppers'** end objective **is to get the best pricing deal and many gorgeous promotional offers to obtain a better shopping experience** and turn them into buyers.

F-Who Is the Consumer?

The consumer is someone who uses a product, commodity, or service regularly. A consumer enters an outlet and goes straight to the shelf and pick up his or her product.
This is also true for organizations, institutions, establishment, and an entity as well.
Those business organizations who have the skill, know-how, expertise, and financial support to influence consumers to buy their products are successful and winners in the market.
For those business organizations to achieve constant growth and gain higher market shares, they have to ensure sustainable growth and profit for their business to offer attractive ROI **for investors.**

G-Understanding Consumer Insight

Understanding consumers' insight in detail will enable a business organization to prosper and achieve the following:

1-**To develop a better product, sales, and marketing strategy.**

2-**To create successful innovations needed for the market.**

3- **To introduce an illustrious advertising strategy.**

4- **To do accurate forecasts and deliver outstanding customer service.**

5- **To present an attractive POS Materials that effectively communicate the displayed products to consumers.**

6- **To provide attractive and desirable promotions to consumers across channels.**

7- **To build credibility by continuously offering valuable information on the stimulus presented to trade.**

8- **To create a productive relationship with consumers by providing quality products with value for money.**

H-What Are The End Objectives Of Shoppers/ Consumers, Retailers, And Brand Owners?

H1-Shoppers/Consumers End Objectives is to get the best pricing deal and lots of promotions to acquire a better shopping experience.

H2-Retailers End Objectives is to give lots of promotions to shoppers and consumers to get high foot traffic and large market baskets.

H3-Brand Owners End Objectives are to provide competitive pricing and many promotions to get brand loyalty and high market shares.

References

1-Shopper Insights – Decision Analysis
https://www.decisionanalyst.com/services/shopperinsights/
2-Shopper Insights vs. Consumer Insights – The Difference – Infosout
https://blog.infoscout.co/shopper-insights-vs-consumer-insights-the-difference/
3-6 Tips for Turning Shoppers Into Buyers – Entrepreneur.com
https://www.entrepreneur.com/article/189404
4-7 Smart Ways Retailers Can Turn "Shoppers" Into "Buyers"
upstreamcommerce.com/blog/2012/09/.../7-smart-ways-retailers-turn-shoppers-buyers
5-What Are Consumer Insights and How Do They Impact
Marketing... https://www.huffingtonpost.com/jure.../what-are-consumer- insight_b_5906624.html
6-Consumer Insights- Most Valuable Consumers-Nielsen
www.nielsen.com/sa/en/solutions/consumer-insights.html
7-Visual Merchandising: How to Display Products In Your Store
https://fitsmallbusiness.com/visual-merchandising-guide/
8- How do I find information about demographics, consumers, and their.
https://johnson.library.cornell.edu/.../how-do-i-find-information-about-demographics-...
9-5 Ways You Can Influence Consumer Purchasing Decision: New.
https://www.socialmediaexaminer.com/5-ways-brands-can-influence-consumer-purch...
10-What is the share of voice – Definition, and Meaning – Business Dictionary
www.businessdictionary.com/definition/share-of-voice.html
11-Consumer Data – Bisnode
https://www.bisnodegroup.com/solutions/enrich-your-data-secure.../consumer-data/
12-Advanced English Dictionary & Thesaurus –
MobiSystemhttps://www.mobisystems.com/advanced-english-dictionary-thesaurus

Preparing An Activity Proposal-Example

A-Sales-force, marketing, and customer development raise activity proposals **to allocate a** budget **for launching a brand, sales, and events. The aim is to achieve sales targets and develop targeted brands, encountering, and blocking competitors' activities. For this, an activity proposal is prepared which consist of the following:**

A1-**Activity proposal number--------**

A2-**Date of the activity and how long it is going to last----------**

A3-**Allocated budget. The cost of the activity ....**

A4-**Participated category or brands. Take for example Fabric Wash** FW as an example.

A5-**Participated** FW **packs by sizes for example** 2.5kg, 4.0kg, and 6.0kg.

B-The Objectives Of The Activities Are As Follow:

B1)-**Achieve** 12% **growth for a Fabric Wash brand over last year.**

B2)-**Attain** 100% **coverage of Winning Trade Outlets** WTO's.

B3)-**Accomplish** 100% **availability of fast-moving packs of the brand during the period of the activity........**

C-The Mechanic Of The Activity

The mechanic of the activity explains **how the objectives of the activity are going to be achieved.
The mechanic is as follows:**

I)-**Last year, in-market sales of Fabric Wash** packs 2.5kg, 4.0kg, 6kg, **was** 41,000 Tons. **Thus,** 12% **annual growth over** the last year will increase from 41,000 Tons to 45,920 Tons. Thus, the new target is 45,920 Tons.

The new target, 45,920 tons will be sold to selected 11,586 winning trade outlets WTO's. Those winning outlets are covered by six branches as stated in detail in below Table

Branch	Number Of WTO's To Be Covered	New Targets by Pack Size by Branch In Ton			
		2.5kg in Ton	4.0 kg in Ton	6.0kg in Ton	Total in Ton
A	1890	1890	2698	3071	7659
B	2005	2458	2896	2657	8011
C	1679	1867	2314	2775	6956
D	2567	2567	2876	2555	7998
E	1354	3012	2987	2103	8102
F	2091	2567	3120	1507	7194
Total	11586	14,361	16,891	14668	45920

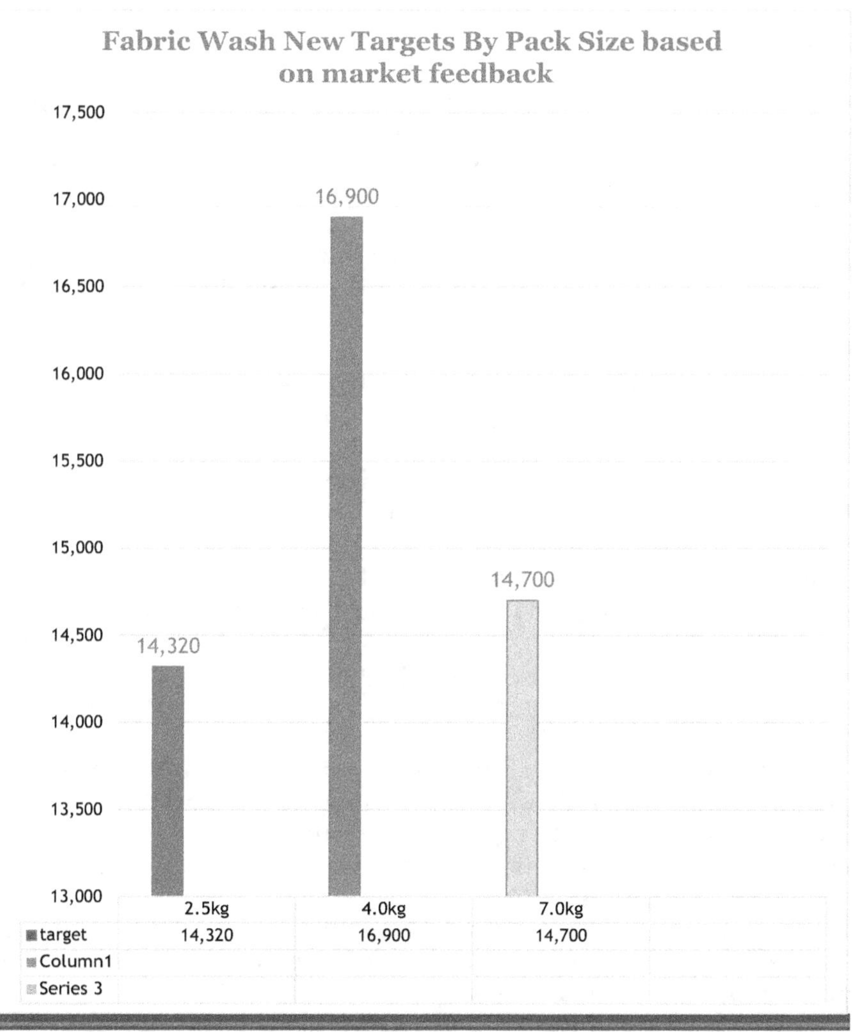

The above figure was based on the market feedback which has indicated that 4kg has the highest sales expectation. Thus, a 4kg pack should get more shelf space, promotions, visibility, and other stimulus activities to reward users, attract new shoppers, and generate higher sales.

<u>**D-Cost Of The Activity**</u>

a) **5% Free Of Cost (FOC) goods will be given to outlets upon buying and displaying Fabric Wash FW packs On the Point Of Purchase POP. The FOC will be given to outlets who achieved their targets by the end of each quarter.**

b) **Also, a visibility contract will be signed with the targeted outlets for extra visibility and floor displays. This is above the 5% FOC that has been given.**

c) **to enhance off-take and to help outlets achieve their targets. Outlets will be supported by various promotions.**

d) **TV commercials on FW will be aired on various prominent TV stations at the best timing during the day.**

<u>**SalesForce Incentive & Cost Break Down**</u>

A-Upon achieving 100% coverage of 11,586 outlets, Sales-force (Sales supervisors + Retail van salesmen will get a bonus equal to USD.......

B-Upon achieving 100% availability of targeted packs, that is every time the outlets are visited, Sales-force will receive a bonus equivalent to USD......

C-Merchandisers will be eligible to receive their bonus upon achieving and maintaining 100% of targeted outlets, visibility at (POP) using required POS materials, as well as floor displays as designated by the activity in a prominent location of WTO's.

D-Branch manager and deputy branch manager will only get their bonus upon achieving 100% of the branch targets. The Recommended bonus is USD...

E-Based on the results of the branches on the activity, the branch with the highest achievement would win the competition between branches and get a Trophy + a bonus of USD .....

F-The activity will be monitored every week to ensure that it is on the right course. In case of deviation from targets is noticed, corrective action would be taken. Further detail on the cost of the activity is reflected in the below table:

<u>**E-Cost Of The Activity In Detail**</u>

Function	Description
Cost of FOC	A free good is given to trade outlets upon achieving their targets.----------
Cost of Sales-force	Bonus is given to sales-force including branch managers & deputy branch managers.----------
Cost of merchandising	All costs related to merchandising of the activity including bonuses given to merchandisers-----------
Cost of visibility	Related costs of the extra visibility made especially for the activity.---------
Cost of promotion	Cost of promotions made for the activity + POSM, leaflets, flags, danglers, and others.-------------
Cost of TV commercials	TV commercial costs created by Fabric Wash made especially for the activity.
Total costs	The total cost of the activity should not exceed 5% of the total revenue.----------

<u>F-Monitoring The Activity</u>

A-11,586 **Covered outlets must** have sufficient **stock before the start of the activity and during the timing of the activity** (Jan-end Dec.). **Placing orders, delivery of the orders on time to winning trade outlets** WTO's and **follow up is the responsibility of the** sales-force and supply chain.

B-**Availability of participated packs in covered outlets must be** 100% **every time those outlets are visited and during the timing of the scheme. This is important and it is also the responsibility of** the sales force covering targeted outlets.

C-**Massive visibility** at POP **and outstanding floor displays in prominent locations of the outlets must be erected, maintained, and monitored through** Jan-end December **by the** merchandising team.

D-**Market feedback on the activity** must be reported daily by the sales force **to ensure compliance and to take action in case of deviation from the activity objectives and mechanics.**

Glossary

1- Achieve
To accomplish or deliver productive results of a business plan on performing given tasks or targets for developing the business of a company, an organization, or trade outlets.

2- Activity
It is a business activity carried out by salesforce in trade outlets aiming to improve sales, achieves successfully set targets, attains greater revenue, and achieve a profit for both trade outlets and the company.

3- Activity Planner
An activity planner is a promotional plan developed by the sales force, customer development team, or marketing.

The activity planner consists of activities by months and by quarters designed to achieve set targets, generate higher sales, encounter competitors' activities, by trade channel, and ensure growth for trade and the company.

4- Activity Proposal
The customer development and marketing raise an activity proposal to allocate a special budget for brand building, increase sales, coverage, distribution, launch a new product, and to encounter competitors.

5- Advertisement
It is a public promotion designed to increase sales for products. The aim is to make those products appealing to consumers, shoppers, and potential buyers. It is an extremely important tool to enhance awareness, generates higher sales, and to accomplish annual sales targets.

6- Assortment
A display arrangement for products by SKU's on the shelf to help consumers and shoppers to select needed pack sizes or variants. It increases sales of assorted products. Assortment provides feedback to the company and trade on the off-take of displayed products by pack size and variant.

7- Cannibalization

To take % sales away and market share from an existing product by a similar but new launched product from the same manufacturer.

8- Category

Similar products are arranged and displayed alongside each other on the shelves based on sameness and similarities to make it easy for consumers and shoppers to see and select.

9- Collaborate

It is a process in which the sales force of the business work as a team with other related business departments in the organization to achieve set targets.

10- Consumer

A Consumer is someone who visits a trade outlet to purchase a brand that is known to him. He uses goods or services regularly.

11- Consumer Insight

To get insight into consumer trends and behavior to provide the right product or service to increase the company's sales and profit.

12- Core Market

The central part of the FMCG's business market which contributes most to the business.

13- Cost Break Down

Details on the cost of the activity step by step vs total revenue generated from the activity which should not be more than 5%.

14- Coverage

The designated number of trade outlets to be covered which are provided with their inquiries in an assigned area by the company's sales force.

15- CU

It is a Consumer Unit if it is available on the shelf with the shelf POSM and is ordered as a regular item. The CU has to have inventory on the shelf at the moment of the measurement.

16- Distribution

The commercial activity of transporting and selling goods and services from producers to customers and consumers. Most large companies such as multinationals use the third party to cover retail and wholesale outlets.

17- Gross Margin

It is the ratio of gross profit divided by sales revenue you may refer to page 55 for further explanation.

18- Investment

Money invested in the business with the expectation to gain profit emerged in the ROI statement.

19- KPI

Business organizations measure their performance against set targets using Key Performance Index KPI.
It is a basis of comparison of achieved results of business activity or annual budget against set targets.

20- Mechanic

The mechanic shows in detail, step by step, how the objective of the business activity is going to be implemented and achieved. It exhibits the process of utilizing the activity to achieve its goals.

21- Method

The method demonstrates systematically step by step ways of implementing a business activity at trade outlets to achieve productive results.

22- Numeric Distribution

The total number of outlets that potentially can sell or buy the company's products. If the number of those outlets is 100 outlet(the universe) and your brand is available in all of them. The Numeric distribution of the brand is 100%

23- OOS

Is Out Of Stock of the consumer unit CU which is in the audit sheet but does not have any inventory on the shelf at the moment of the measurement.

24- OSA

Is On Shelf Availability which is having the right product on the right shelf at the right time of the time of measurement.

25- Point Of Purchase (POP)

POP is an area on the shelf designated for the same products to be displayed next to each other. Companies are competing with each other to have more faces for their products on the Point Of Purchase POP to influence shoppers & consumers to pick up their products.

26- Quality

Referring to the quality of the product which is going to be sold to consumers, shoppers, and customers. The product should be seen as a superior and with a high degree of excellence. The product is seen as by those who buy it as good value for the money paid for it.

27- Sales Force

The division of a business which is responsible for selling products or services.

28- Scarcity

Demand is high for a product but it is only available in limited quantity in the market.

29- Scheme

A scheme is a systematic course of action or a plan offering trade channels gifts or price discounts. The scheme aims to generate higher revenue, increase coverage, growth, distribution, and achieve set targets.

30- Shopper

A shopper may visit outlets and not buying any item. Sampling and promotions offered on brands in outlets may turn shoppers into buyers.

31- SKU's

Stock Keeping Unit SKU's. It is counted as the company inventory of products, brands available by pack sizes, and variants.

32- Stock

The number of goods available in the company's warehouses ready to be sold to trade outlets. This is true for trade outlets as well.

33- Strategy

A detailed systematic clear plan of action for a designated period to be implemented to achieve a goal.

34- Survey

A detailed critical inspection of available alternatives to get the best course of action aiming to achieve growth for the business.

35- Sustainability

The ability to maintain success in the market is based on understanding the process of change and the exploitation of resources efficiently.

36- SWOT

It is Strengths, Weaknesses, Opportunity, and Threat. Analysis of the position of your business vs competitors, the environment, and the economy.

37- TPR

Temporary Price Reduction TPR. The TPR is offered to trade to increase sales to achieve set targets.

38- Trade Channel

According to the market structure of FMCG's, they are hypermarkets, supermarkets, large groceries, groceries, pharmacies, perfumeries, wholesalers, and other FMCG's outlets.

39- Trade Drive Scheme

The scheme aims to increase sales by providing trade outlets incentives based on agreed growth targets by both trade and the company.

40- Weighted Distribution

Covering only Important outlets that contribute a high percentage, more than 80% of the business. Focusing on those outlets achieve solid coverage and distribution as well as saving cost.

41- Winning Trade Outlets WTO's

Trade outlets that are growing in the market continuously and have a high potential to achieve higher growth for the company's brands in the coming years.

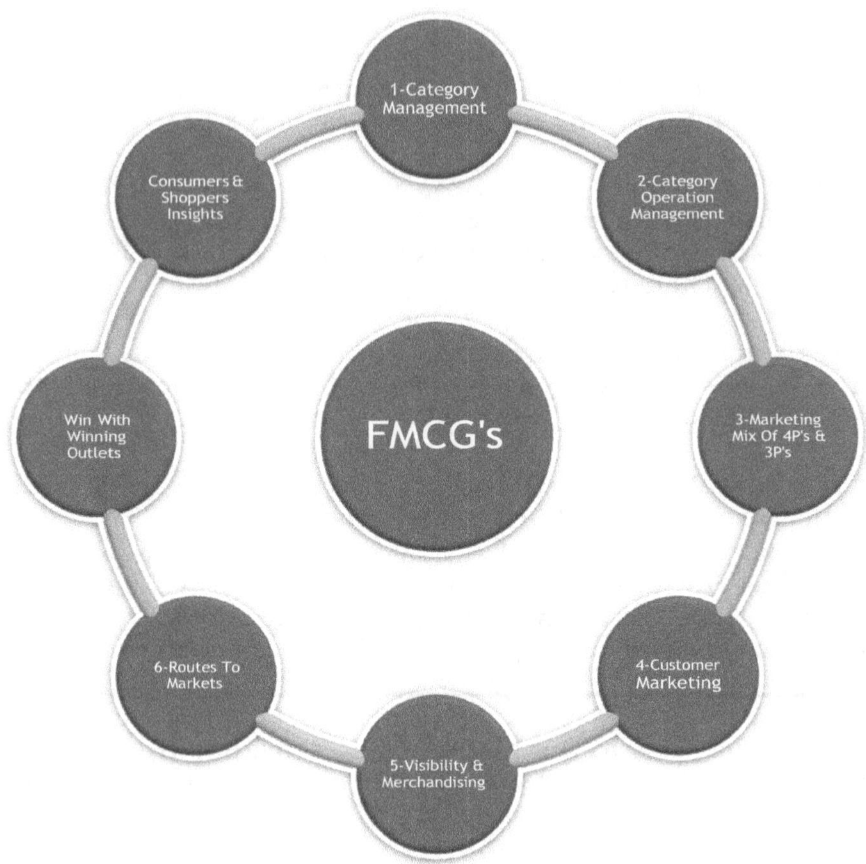

The primary objective of every company large or small is to manage its business successfully, achieve its target year on year, obtain higher market shares for its brands, secure sustainable growth, offer attractive Return On Investment ROI to investors, and be friendly with the environment. For the company to reach such an important goal successfully, it has to understand and implement the eight principles of the FMCG's stated above and make them work in coordination and harmony with each other as one unit across all the functions of the eight principles of FMCG'

www.ingramcontent.com/pod-product-compliance
Lightning Source LLC
LaVergne TN
LVHW050642200726
843506LV00010B/1328